The TRUTH about LYING

How to Spot a Lie
and Protect Yourself from Deception

The TRUTH about LYING

How to Spot a Lie and Protect Yourself from Deception

Stan B. Walters

SOURCEBOOKS, INC.®
NAPERVILLE, ILLINOIS

This publication is designed to provide accurate and authoritative information in regard to the subject matter covered. It is sold with the understanding that the publisher is not engaged in rendering legal, accounting, or other professional service. If legal advice or other expert assistance is required, the services of a competent professional person should be sought.—*From a Declaration of Principles Jointly Adopted by a Committee of the American Bar Association and a Committee of Publishers and Associations*

Published by Sourcebooks, Inc.

P.O. Box 4410, Naperville, Illinois 60567-4410

(630) 961-3900

FAX: (630) 961-2168

Library of Congress Cataloging-in-Publication Data

Walters, Stan B.

The truth about lying: how to spot a lie and protect yourself from deception/ Stan Walters.

     p. cm.

   Includes index

    ISBN 1-57071-511-4 (pbk. : alk. paper)

1.Deception. 2. Truthfulness and falsehood. I. Title.

BF637.D42 W35 2000

363.25'4—dc21

                                        00-024735

Printed and bound in the United States of America

VHG   10 9 8 7 6 5 4 3 2 1

Dedication

In memory of my dad, W. Louis Walters

1919–1999

A man of character, honor, compassion, integrity, and faith.

Acknowledgments

There are always a lot of people working behind the scenes who help smooth the way and make a project like this a reality. Thanks to Michelle Banks of Maxwell Media Group, who kept after me, encouraged me, and got the ball rolling. My gratitude and thanks to my editor, Deborah Werksman of Sourcebooks, whose talents are many, whose patience is endless, and who put the polish and shine to my humble efforts. My good friend Jim Alsup, the Director of Public Agency Training Council, who always has an eye to the future and all its possibilities. Special thanks to Dr. Martha Davis, Principal Researcher, and the great folks at John Jay College of Criminal Justice and our very dedicated and diligent research team.

My never-ending love and thanks to Hilda, my best friend, partner, and wife, who knows how to bring out the best in me and who always shares my dreams and schemes. Her encouragement and support makes me think all things are possible. And to Hilary, Allison, and Jordan, my two daughters and granddaughter, who ask little, tolerate a lot, and deserve the best from their dad and "Pepaw."

Table of Contents

Chapter One: What's Behind a Lie **1**

Chapter Two: Guidelines and Principles **29**

Chapter Three: Verbal Communication **59**

Chapter Four: Nonverbal Communication **75**

Chapter Five: Response Behavior **111**

Chapter Six: Using What You Know **165**

End Notes **173**

Bibliography **177**

Index **189**

About the Author **195**

What's

BEHIND a LIE

What's

BEHIND a LIE

Chapter One

H

ave you ever been talking to someone and had a gut feeling that the person was lying to you? You just had the sense that something was not right, but maybe you couldn't quite put your finger on any particular thing the person said or did that made you uneasy. Have you ever placed your trust in someone and later found out that he had been lying to you? Have you ever watched and listened to a conversation between two other people and you "knew" that one was lying to the other, and the poor victim bought everything the other person said, hook, line, and sinker?

When was the last time you lied to someone? Maybe you just didn't tell that person everything or didn't give a complete answer. Maybe you just "fibbed" to him. You might even have called it "a little white lie," but it was a lie just the same. Did you allow someone to make the wrong assumption because of what you did or did not tell him? Perhaps you didn't intend to mislead him but he just came to the wrong conclusion. Congratulations! You lied to someone!

We are faced with deception all around us. Either we are being lied to or we lie to someone else. It is not always done with malicious or evil intent. It is not necessarily covering up a crime or committing perjury. It may be fudging a little on job or loan applications. It may be protecting someone's feelings by not saying exactly what you think about the clothes he chooses, his new haircut, the decorating style, or his new girlfriend. Maybe you have decided that your friend needs to learn the hard way, or you'd prefer he find out the truth from someone else. You don't want to be the one to deliver the bad news. At other times, maybe you just need to explain away why you're really late for work or why the work you did is late. And of course, everyone embellishes a little when out on a date—especially a first date. The dating ritual itself must be the most frequent form of deception people ever commit!

Remember here that we're not talking about criminals but about upstanding, everyday people, including yourself. The very fabric of culture is woven from what many consider harmless lies, such as excuses made for declining an invitation, or compliments that aren't what you really believe.

The problem is that every day of your life you make decisions after considering numerous pieces of information, facts, and opinions that you gather from the people around you—decisions that affect the lives and future of your family, friends, business associates, and yourself. You make those decisions based on the belief that those who provide the information are reliable and trustworthy and have your best interests at heart. But what if those people upon whom you rely, from whom you seek information and guidance, are not truthful with you? What if, instead of having your best interests at heart, they were more interested in serving their own personal interests and goals? If you knew from the outset that someone upon whom you relied was not being honest with you and was misleading you, withholding information from you, or being evasive about the truth, would it make any difference in the decisions you made? Can you afford to make a critical decision, or even a simple day-to-day decision, only to find out later that it was based on false or misleading information?

As a general rule, human beings do a very poor job of detecting deception. You might be surprised to learn that law enforcement investigators don't do any better than the general public in their ability to accurately spot a liar. How can we miss such behavior when we do the same thing ourselves? Are there any tell-tale signs? Are there any symptoms that can help us spot deception among our spouses, friends, family members, business associates, or politicians? Aren't there some special clues we can look for? Isn't there anything we can do to stop others from lying to us?

In reality, there is little if anything you can do to stop someone from lying to you. You must accept the fact that people at some time are going to lie to you. This is not a condemnation of the human race, nor should you become suspicious and paranoid. But the fact that someone may attempt to deceive you does not mean that you have to be a victim of his deception. The best thing you can do to protect yourself is to learn how to do a better job of recognizing and correctly identifying the complex behaviors that are associated with human communication. You can learn to hear the changes in the voice and understand the meaning of

You cannot stop someone from lying to you, but you can avoid being a victim of his lies.

the subtle nuances associated with the rate of speech, pitch of the voice, and volume that can tip you off to deception. Listening to the content of speech can help you to understand the specific mechanisms at work within the mind of the person to whom you are listening. If you can learn how to look past the distractions of stress and disguise that are found in body language, you can more accurately decipher the meaning of gestures, posture, positions, expressions, and movements.

You certainly cannot expect to isolate and identify every single lie that you might witness, but, if you could identify the majority of the numerous attempts at deception that are made around you everyday, how much better would your life and personal relationships be? How much personal pain and loss could you avoid if you knew how to correctly decode the verbal and nonverbal communications of those with whom you associate? Then you would be able to communicate in such a way as to encourage open, honest dialogue, and you could create an environment of trust and trustworthiness around yourself so as to improve your relationships.

You cannot and never will be able to stop someone from lying to you, but you can avoid being a victim to lies of others by acquiring the skills to correctly assess the credibility of another person's statements. Human behavior and communications studies that have focused on deception indicate the behaviors that are reliable when it comes to diagnosing someone's credibility and those behaviors that are not dependable because they are based on nothing more than folk wisdom. By establishing guidelines and a basic set of principles on how to recognize those significant behaviors, you can reduce the chances that you will mislabel innocent behaviors or fail to recognize the verbal and nonverbal phenomenon that would alert you that someone is trying to deceive you.

Furthermore, if you can look critically at yourself and understand your own actions and reactions, emotions and motivations, thoughts and fears, and the image you have of yourself and what you want others to see in you, then you will begin to understand why others have chosen to try to deceive you and why you have deceived them.

These skills will be useful to you in all kinds of situations with people offering you their services, such as a nanny or a car mechanic, with people selling you their products, and with friends and members of your family. You'll be in a better position to make those important decisions in your life when you know what makes people lie to you, how to tell when they may be lying, and different techniques for dealing with a lie when you believe you have been confronted by one. You also may want to apply these skills to drawing your own conclusions about what you see on the news or read about in the newspaper.

Let me emphasize here that it is at all times my intention to help you develop these skills so that they can have a positive impact on your life and your relationships. It would be a shame if, after reading this book, you suddenly became suspicious and distrustful of your mate, children, friends, and the person on the street. It is my belief that knowing how to recognize deception can give you a chance to uncover areas in your life and relationships you can positively impact.

Defining Deception

Obfuscate. Misinform. Mislead. Dissemble. Prevaricate. Muddle. Deceive. Fabricate. Cloak. Distort. Equivocate. Fib. Invent. Falsify. Misrepresent. Adulterate. Evade. Hedge. Spin. Lie. Deception by whatever name is still an attempt by a person to deceive not only someone else but also himself into the bargain. We all have, or will, engage in at least some subtle form of deception on a daily basis. Some of these attempts to deceive are malicious in nature while other occurrences are more in the form of editing, which is designed to preserve feelings, a relationship, or the current communication exchange that has been established between two or more people. Let's face it: sometimes people, including you and me, would much rather hear subtle distortions of the truth than to hear the blunt, cold, hard reality.

The presence of deception in any instance suggests that the speaker has found some need to alter the perception of the truth. For the target of the deception, you the listener, the reasons behind that deception may be of vital importance in your decision-making process regarding the issue at hand and your perception of the other person's credibility and integrity. Why has the person felt it necessary to be deceitful to you? To get a better grasp on deception, you need to understand the internal systems at work when someone is being deceptive.

Three factors or conditions exist in any situation where deception is occurring: choice, opportunity, and ability. If you understand these three factors, you can get a better handle on why and how deception occurs, how to recognize it, and how to reduce the chances that it will occur in your presence.

Choice

Choice is one of the key factors that exists whenever lying takes place. The person reasons or feels that there is pressure on him not to tell the whole and complete truth, and so he chooses to lie in some form. He may feel a need to lie in order to gain some form of reward or positive reinforcement that he desires. He may feel that a lie or half-truth will help him to avoid some form of punishment or negative reinforcement. Finally, he may feel pressured to deceive out of fear or an inability to determine what the consequences of the conversation may be. You as the target of the deceit may have little or no impact at all on the subject's choice to lie.

Lying is a cognitive, or mental, process. It is not something that merely happens in a vacuum. To mislead or misinform others is a deliberate action and it is a behavior in which one chooses to engage. By being deceptive, a person accomplishes some goal, whether it be to gain a personal benefit, to avoid some form of unattractive consequence, or to protect himself or someone else in a situation that appears to be unpredictable. My point here is that a decision is made every time a lie occurs, and there are countless situations in which a person may choose to lie.

In fact, almost everyone has a boundary, or a code of honor beyond which he will not go. In other words, a person might be unwilling to lie to his spouse, but lying to the IRS might be acceptable. Parents often are willing to hide information from their children, but would never do so in an interaction with their boss.

The more that a person perceives is at stake, the more pressure he may feel to choose to be deceitful. For a teenager, this may be nothing more than the chance to go out on Friday or Saturday night when asked about where he's going and with whom. It can, of course, be a much more serious situation involving, with our hypothetical teenager, drugs, alcohol, or shoplifting, or with an adult, tax evasion or a political cover-up. My point is that regardless of the circumstances, there is always a choice made somewhere along the way.

We could get into a long psychological, philosophical, and moral discussion about character, socialization, and self-esteem issues exploring why a person chooses to lie, but we are going to leave the majority of that discussion to other forums. The decision to be deceitful is one that is made solely by a person who has lied and that decision was made consciously and deliberately. One is almost never "forced" to lie except in extreme circumstances. Since we are dealing in this book with everyday situations, it is rarely the case that a person will be "forced" to lie to you, although he may perceive a need to do so.

A lie is always by choice, not by accident.

Ability

A person's ability to lie and to lie well rests squarely on his communication skills and intellectual powers. This is not to suggest that people with good communication skills are going to be more deceptive than others, but if they choose to be, they may have more of an advantage. Others, lacking the strong communication skills to bolster the ability to be deceptive, may have to work harder at it. Unfortunately, to some, lying almost seems to come naturally.

Opportunity

If someone can communicate well and is inclined to be deceitful, there is little you can do. The only one of the key factors of lying over which you may have some control is the opportunity for the person to lie. To avoid being the intended target of a lie, you may want to create the impression that you are an undesirable target for someone else's deception. You can do this by making it unrewarding for someone to lie to you, developing the skills necessary to spot a lie, and learning how to challenge lies when they occur. You will reduce the opportunities that others have to lie to you, reduce the likelihood that they will take the opportunity to lie if one does arise, and minimize the extent of damage to yourself that a lie could cause if they do take the opportunity.

The only one of the key factors of lying over which you have some control is the opportunity for the person to lie.

Responsibility

Many times, we have a sense or feeling that someone may be lying to us but we lack the skills necessary to pinpoint exactly which behaviors make us feel that way. In the absence of confirming information, or the knowledge we need to decide if the person is being deceptive, we defer to how we feel about the person.

When it is a person you know well, you may rely on the strength of your past encounters and the length of the relationship. You may make a snap judgment if you are feeling angry with the person at that moment or if you are feeling compassionate. If it is a person who is a relative stranger, you may rely on gut instinct or on the person's "vibe," or your perception of the energy he is giving out.

You always will rely on these feelings to some extent, but if you take the time to understand and master the methods in this book, you will have a great deal more information on which to base your conclusions; you'll also have a number of options to choose from in deciding how you want to handle the situation. Remember, this book is all about improving your relationships, not disrupting them.

When a person is trying to deceive someone, one of the concerns that eventually arises is the vulnerability of that person to being deceived. If the liar believes that the person is very competent at spotting lies, one or two reactions may occur within the liar. One response may be that under the stress of scrutiny the liar ends up generating even more recognizable signs of deceit. The second response may be that the deceiver reconsiders the choice to lie. The end result either way is that the lies are more easily exposed or fewer lies are generated. Your best weapon in denying a person the opportunity to lie to you is learning how to accurately spot the signals of deception. By detecting deception accurately on a regular basis, you will make yourself a less favorable target for deceit.

The second thing you must do is be willing to look at your own role in a situation where someone is lying to you. Do you make it difficult for people to tell you the truth as they see it because you react emotionally? Do you violently express hurt feelings? Do you become angry or vengeful? Are you known as someone who is easily offended? Do you punish your children if they admit they've done something wrong? No matter how good you get at detecting a lie, you will be setting yourself up to be lied to if people are afraid to tell you the truth. In a situation not involving someone close to you, such as when you are hiring someone to provide a service to you, are you careful and diligent in hiring, or are you quick and impulsive and always looking for the quickest solution? Are you willing to spend a little more time and learn more about this person who is offering you a service or a product, be it a lawyer, an insurance salesman, or a car mechanic? Do you have the time to make careful observations, ask thoughtful questions, and think carefully about what you observed?

> **You must be willing to look at your own role in a situation where someone is lying to you.**

No matter how well you remember the information in this book, if you are not willing to look at your own role in your encounters with other people—Did I look angry when my teenager came in late? Was I in such a hurry to buy that insurance that I didn't shop around?— if you are examining only the other person, you are getting only half the equation. In fact, as we'll discuss later, your actions can even affect the signals a person gives off, thereby making it harder for you to evaluate those signals. That is called "contamination" and we'll be looking at it more closely later on.

Communicating Your Findings

As a general rule, it is better not to tell people about their signs of deception. As you learn to use the various analysis techniques we are discussing, you may be tempted to tell a person that you have caught him lying and tell him specifically which behavior symptoms gave him away. If that's the case, there are a lot of people who are going to want to play poker with you because you have shown your hand! It may seem like a good idea and you may believe that it puts extra pressure on the person you are observing, but in the long run you are hurting yourself for several reasons.

First, once you tell the person what you have identified as deceptive, you may not ever see that person exhibit that behavior again. You have just alerted him to exactly how you've spotted his deception and now he will try to suppress that specific behavior or behaviors. Second, once the person has been told what tell-tale behaviors have given him away, he may try to mask those signs by acting out substitute symptoms or by staging the behavior you have identified as a feint when telling the truth. This is an attempt to destroy your confidence in the accuracy of your diagnosis. Granted, you may not believe that anyone will be able to have such control of his own behavior or have the presence of mind to be able to accomplish such a feat, but the reality is that all you have succeeded in doing is to make the work harder and more complex for yourself.

It is better not to tell others about their signs of deception.

Finally, pointing out these behaviors to people is bound to have a negative effect on your family, social life, and business life. No one likes to have attention called to his weaknesses or personal flaws. Calling attention to someone's deceptive behaviors will most certainly contaminate the behaviors of others around you who will then feel you are scrutinizing their statements and analyzing them for deception. It is fine for you to develop your skills in identifying deceptive behavior without trumpeting to all who know you that you are now a human "lie detector." Think of it as learning how to use tools that will improve your own communication skills. The ability to identify when a person you're talking to is experiencing stress in the conversation, and may be considering if it is safe to tell you the truth, will give you an opportunity to create an atmosphere in which people can be honest with you about what is on their minds. This will be invaluable to you in your personal relationships. In situations where the person is a stranger to you and you are considering goods or services, these skills will help you identify when you'll want to dig for more information, check another reference, shop around a little more. Throughout this book, I'll discuss what tactics you can take when you are sure you've identified a deception. By the end of this book, you'll know not only how to spot a lie, but what to do about it.

Defining Evasion

Direct deception, as we have described previously, involves actively changing or altering the truth. The only thing that will limit a person's ability to engage effectively in this form of deception is his own imagination. Alternatively, a person can accomplish his deception by engaging in the indirect method of deception—evasion. When being evasive, the deceiver merely withholds from the listener, rather than changes, critical information. Evasion has some advantages and disadvantages for the deceiver.

Evasion is the indirect method of deception.

One advantage of using the indirect method of deception is that it is not a demanding or daunting mental process. For direct deception to be successful, I must remember previous lies, create new lies that are consistent with the older ones, and leave the new lies vague and open-ended enough in case I have to change them or add onto them later. When I use evasion, I don't have to remember what I've said, because I'm not actively creating alternate or misleading information. When I'm lying through evasion, I am simply leaving out information from the communication process.

Another advantage to evasion is that what I do say is going to be the truth. Since the information I am conveying to the listener is based on the truth, I will have a generally easy time maintaining a handle on the important or significant information. I won't have to sort between truth and the web of lies I have created in order to respond to any questions. I merely edit out or remove selected information from my account of the situation or experience.

For deception by evasion to be successful, I must have some idea of how much you need to know in order to feel as though you have gotten the truth. Then, I must carefully select what to tell you. My aim is to reveal only some of the facts and let you assume the rest. I want to give you enough to satisfy you, when in reality, I have given you only enough so that you will come to the wrong conclusion. I know that you have drawn the wrong conclusion by the nature of your questions and the content of your remarks, but I do nothing to correct you and my deceit through evasion has been a success. The story of the city slicker and the dog is a great example of this method in action.

A traveler has been driving through the country on a trip and stops for lunch in a small town. Taking a walk in the courthouse square, he sees an old farmer sitting on a park bench, reading a newspaper. Sitting beside him is an interesting looking dog. The traveler walks over, sits down next to the farmer, and tries to strike up a friendly conversation. The farmer, wary of strangers, does little more than grunt short answers to the traveler's questions. "My, that is a very interesting looking dog," says the city slicker. "I had a dog just like that when I was a kid." The old farmer just nods in silent response. "He looks like a pretty good dog to me," says the city slicker. The farmer silently nods. "Does your dog bite?" asks the city slicker. "Nope," answers the old farmer. "Do you mind if I pet the dog?" asks the city slicker. "Nope," answers the farmer. The traveler reaches out his hand out to pet the animal. The dog snarls and snaps at the stranger, taking a big bite out of the poor man's hand. In pain and shock, he yells at the old farmer, "I thought you said your dog doesn't bite!" "My dog don't bite," responds the farmer. "Well, then look what your dog just did to my hand!" shouts the wounded man. "That ain't my dog," responds the grinning farmer.

Although evasion seems more of a "not doing" than "doing" process, the indirect deception technique of evasion does place some demands on the liar. First, the deceiver must know the truth in order to be able to censor certain parts of that information from his remarks or conversation.

Second, it is critical that the evader knows just how much information to give to the person whom he hopes to mislead. There is a very delicate balance between too much information and not enough to allow for misinterpretation. If the deceiver says just a little too much, the truth may come out. If he doesn't say enough, it will be obvious that he is holding back on providing all of the information. The evader must pay attention to his listener's responses and gauge the success of his efforts to deceive. This method of deception requires a liar who is skilled in the art of communication because he must know exactly what to say and when. More important, he must know when to keep his mouth shut!

Dealing with Evasion

Detecting lies of evasion or omission is not easy for the listener who is the intended victim. Direct deception is much easier to spot because there is some material to work with: the other person's lies or made-up version of the truth, as well as the symptoms of stress and deception he exhibits as he tries to make all of the pieces of the story work together. When dealing with indirect deception, however, you have to be able to spot the deceit by using logic instead of observation. You have to recognize that the transition of events described from one point of the conversation to the next has some missing elements. It helps if you already know some of the facts, because you may realize that the other person's answers aren't giving you the whole story. Additionally, during this type of conversation you cannot assume anything, because the liar wants you to do just that—make an incorrect assumption. Instead, you will have to question tediously the person about every element that you feel is vague or incomplete and pull the information out of him one piece at a time, only believing what you know to be true.

Deal with evasion by asking direct or indirect questions.

Depending on the person you are talking to, you may want to ask direct questions, or you may want to ask questions in a more roundabout manner. You may want to state the assumption you think he wants you to make, and then see if that is correct. When faced with such a direct question, the evader will either have to lie outright or have to be more forthcoming. If he begins to lie outright, you will then be able to apply the skills you will learn in this book to uncover the lie.

Motivations for Deceit or Evasion

When a person chooses to be deceitful or evasive, he is doing so for one of two main reasons. First, he may wish to mislead you regarding some event that has occurred in the past and thereby keep you from learning the truth. Second, he may wish to accomplish a hidden agenda going forward.

When I lie to you about something that has happened in the past, I do so primarily to avoid some form of punishment. Your disappointment in me may be punishment enough. This is often the case with young people who don't want their parents to find out about youthful indiscretions. Or, I may fear that you finding out about my actions could destroy the image you have of me and who I am. That image may be one that I have worked hard to develop. This can happen among friends when there might be a concern that the future relationship will suffer or in a business situation when you might decline to hire me if you know about something that happened in the past. If the acts I have committed and tried to hide are of a serious enough nature, I may fear for my job, my marriage, my public title, or even my freedom should you discover what I have done.

For example, a businessman who has lost investors' money through imprudence or a high-profile public figure who has had an inappropriate sexual encounter with one of his staff may very well compound his errors by virtue of a cover-up. On the other hand, I may plan to deceive you not about something I have done in the past, but about something I am presently doing or hope to do. In this case, I have some clear objective, and if you were aware of it, you might interfere with my plans. My deceit is an effort at creating an illusion. I wish you to believe in what you think you see or what you expect to have happen.

For example, a teenager might want to go to a party that all of his friends are attending, but he knows his parents would disapprove. In order to get out of the house, he tells his parents he is going over to a friend's house, and perhaps out to the movies, to prevent them from calling there to locate him. When his parents tell him that he is not to go anywhere else, he swears to them that he is not going to the party. He may act insulted and complain that they just don't trust him.

Take another example in which a person is selling a car because the transmission has been acting up and he doesn't want to pay for any more repairs. As you are looking over the car, you ask about its mechanical condition—the gas mileage, if the car uses oil, or if it has ever been in an accident. The seller may choose not to tell you about the transmission problems because you didn't ask directly, and he doesn't want to discourage you from pursuing the car's purchase.

Deception and evasion each serves its own purpose, and to be realistic, most people have engaged in each type at some point or another. We also have been victims of the same. We may encounter deception or evasion from a family member or close friend, from a co-worker or a relative stranger. How we deal with it, and how we detect it, will be different depending on how close to us the person is.

Defining Stress

Our lives are composed of a series of goals and objectives. We strive to accomplish these goals and objectives on both a daily and a long-term basis. The nature of each of those goals represents what is truly important to us and tells others a lot about who we are. They are what motivate us to behave the way we do. Some of the objectives are complex and serve as outlines for such fundamental decisions as how we want to represent ourselves to others or to which spiritual and religious principles we will adhere. Other goals are simple and are limited to bowling a perfect game or breaking par on a tough hole at the local golf course. The important thing to keep in mind is not so much the level of complexity of the goal or objective, but more of how highly we value its achievement and how vigorously we pursue its successful fulfillment. Any real or perceived threats to our ability either to pursue or to accomplish these goals and objectives can create emotional and intellectual discord within us. That tension is commonly referred to as stress.

We experience stress on three levels—physical, emotional, and mental. Physical symptoms can include perspiration, stomach cramps, dilated pupils, rapid and shallow breath, or slow and deep inhalations. Our faces may flush and our muscles might become taut as we prepare for fight or flight. Our hands may begin to tremble; our balance may become unsteady, and our face may blanch. Emotionally, we may experience fear or anger. At the same time, we experience significant mental changes, which can include confusion, rapid or disjointed thoughts, intense concentration, forgetfulness, or even hallucinations.

Unresolved stress can cause many types of physical and psychological problems. You may have read something about the damaging effects stress can have on the body. It can cause extreme weight loss, hair loss, high blood pressure, headaches, backaches, muscle aches, muscle twitches, ringing in the ears, heart attacks, strokes, intestinal disorders, rashes, joint pain, chronic sickness, or chronic fatigue syndrome. We could also suffer from emotional disorders such as depression, personality disorders, long-term or short-term memory problems, paranoia, and anger management problems; we may even become psychotic or mentally disturbed. All of these problems are caused by either major chemical changes in the body or by emotional confusion and distress, both of which result from excessive and prolonged stress.

The interesting thing about stress is its true source. Throughout our lives, we receive, in a continual series, rewards and punishments. Through personal experiences over time, we learn which of our behaviors will earn rewards and which ones will create the negative feedback associated with punishment. We adjust our lives on the basis of our perceptions of how to maximize rewards and minimize punishments. In some cases, however, we may not know exactly

Signs of stress may or may not signal deception.

what the result of our choice will be. We make a decision assuming it will have a positive outcome, but instead it may turn out badly. When this happens, we must choose between the options of fight or flight. At the same time, we must attend to the stress we are experiencing because our plans didn't work out as expected.

We all experience some form of stress in our daily lives. Perhaps we are having trouble getting the lawnmower started on the first try when we want to cut the grass before the rain begins. Maybe a do-it-yourself home repair project is not going very well: "It looked so simple when that couple did it on the television home improvement show. Why won't it work for me?" You could find that you have a flat tire on the way to pick up your child from daycare. Maybe you are having company over for dinner but you still have to do some last minute cleaning, get one more dish prepared, and need to take a shower and get dressed before the guests arrive. Or, there are the flashing red and blue lights of a police car right behind you as you are speeding in an effort to get to work on time. For the most part, these types of events create what is called general stress.

What is the actual cause of this stress? Are there external forces? Does it spring from an internal source? Is it the workload at your job that causes stress? How about that one supervisor who seems to be overly critical of your performance, is he the root of your stress? Are you stressed by the fact that your son is in college and you are spending a fortune on tuition, but you don't think he is as dedicated to his studies as you think he should be? Do the time constraints and complicated tax forms that you struggle with each year give you stress? The answer is, no. That's right, none of these situations cause stress. What really is creating your stress are your thoughts about each of those problems. The Greek philosopher Epictetus said, "Men are not troubled by things themselves, but by their thoughts about them." When we dwell on a problem with too much intensity or for too long, our thoughts about the frustrations associated with that issue are responsible for our feelings of being overwhelmed.

The stress phenomenon that we are going to use for the diagnosis of a person's deceptive behaviors comes from the general category of stress reactions. It is important to bear in mind, however, that this does not mean that anyone who is experiencing some form of stress is lying. All deception signals, either verbal or nonverbal, are a form of stress, but not all stress signs indicate lying. Were you ever extremely nervous during a job interview or when reciting a poem in front of the class in high school? You weren't lying; you were anxious about getting the job or intimidated by standing in front of the class.

The stress that occurs when you are being deceptive has some additional elements to it. You still exhibit all of the other typical stress symptoms, such as sweating, absentmindedly wringing your hands, crossing your arms, or talking in a high-pitched voice. The difference occurs in the origin of the stress and subsequent symptoms. We may generate our deception cues because we have strong, personal feelings about the issue, and we do not want the other person to discover our true feelings. Or the reverse may be true in that we want the observer to think we are experiencing a particular emotion that we, in fact, don't genuinely feel. To complete our deception, we must give a good enough performance so that the other person doesn't realize an emotional incongruity exists. Concern over whether the other person believes our deceptive performance is the cause of our stress.

The stress associated with deception is generated by the conflict between the truth and our own portrayal of reality. Knowing the truth about a matter and presenting it in an altered form by changing some or all of the facts creates a problem. The lying person has to be actively involved in editing and censoring his remarks, and the failure to do so exposes him to a great deal of risk. The stress he experiences is the result of heightened mental activity as he monitors his speech amid increased concern that the observer will be able to decipher the truth.

All forms of stress come back to the main issue of rewards and punishments. If I fail at my deceit, what is the punishment for engaging in fabrication? What would be the costs I have to pay for failing? How significantly will I be set back in my efforts to achieve my ultimate goals or objectives? Could I be denied completely that goal forever, or could I recover? Is the goal so important that I will risk everything to attain it? Am I willing to throw caution to the wind, pull out all the stops, and make the ultimate sacrifices at all costs to achieve that goal? Such is the dilemma of engaging in deception.

Most of the time, you will be recognizing signs of stress that may or may not signal deception. It will be useful to you to observe to yourself, "A ha! This person is experiencing stress in this conversation." You can then begin to communicate with that person about what his agenda is—if you can uncover his goals, you will be in a position to understand his motivations and communicate with him in a constructive way.

Relationships

We can classify the people with whom we deal in our daily lives into four general categories—intimate, personal, social, and public. Each of these groups has a different meaning to us and we maintain different types of relationships with each. People in our lives may also move from one category to another, as well.

Intimate

The intimate group consists of those people with whom we maintain a very close relationship. They are most likely to know the most about our personal goals and dreams as well as our successes and failures. They are equally likely to have shared with us the depths of emotional pain and the greatest joys. In fact, most of the time they are active participants in those events. This group of people includes parents, spouses, children, siblings, extended family, lovers, spiritual counselors, and, in some cases, especially close friends or those who closely fill one of these roles.

Dishonesty among the members of the intimate group can create a great deal of emotional pain. The deceiver has betrayed those who have placed trust and confidence in him. Should a member of the group fail to meet the group's expectations, there would be disappointment in the failure but ultimately that person probably would be forgiven. Blatant dishonesty, however, creates a wound that will be difficult to heal. The unwritten rule between the members of the intimate group is that there is ultimate trust between the members. We all are honest with each other and will faithfully defend and support each other. Each person has willingly exposed his innermost self to the others at great risk, but with the understanding that he will be accepted unconditionally, warts and all. To deceive someone in my intimate circle for selfish reasons, or while knowing that that person will be personally

Dishonesty among the members of the intimate group can create a great deal of emotional pain.

harmed by my deceit, creates a huge rift between the liar and the deceived. We risk the greatest of all punishments for such a transgression—the loss of love. And it can be more difficult to disguise deception, because these are the people who know each other best and are most likely to read the true meanings of behaviors and see through lies. Working in the deceiver's favor, however, can be the unwillingness that intimates may have to believe something bad about one of their own. Even when the lies are badly executed, the deceiver may get away with them in a dysfunctional situation.

Personal

The group of people that compose my personal circle would include my close friends, a small group of people with whom I regularly associate on a casual basis. It might be a few people at work, college buddies, or members of a sports team. It might be the group with whom I go to parties or the couple that my spouse and I spend time with on a regular basis. This group has a different set of rules than those of the intimate group.

When deception occurs between the members of this group, a great deal depends on the type of deception. Perhaps I'm always telling the war stories that seem to grow a little more unbelievable each time. These are little lies that may be generally allowed as part of the group behavior. If, however, I betray a trust with a member of the group, I could lose that person as a friend. I could also sacrifice the friendship and closeness of the relationship if my deceit is for personal gain at his expense.

When deception occurs between the members of this group, a great deal depends on the type of deception.

If I'm caught deceiving a member of the personal group, I may have that person angry at me for a long time and in the future he may be more careful in his dealings with me. If my deception of that person is significant enough, the entire group may shun me for what I have done. As a result, I may find it very difficult ever to be allowed to be close to members of that group. Deceit within the personal group can cause a fair amount of emotional pain, but unlike the intimate group, relationships in this group may not be considered to be lifelong relationships anyway. Over long periods of time, friends come and go as people grow and change. Being out of touch with a former friend is unlikely to be as painful as estrangement from a sibling, parent, or spouse.

Social

The social group is composed of those individuals with whom I associate on a temporary basis. Often we do not have much at stake in our relationship except for very limited situations. This may be the members of the congregation at my church. I recognize them and they know who I am. These are people I recognize at the grocery store, the people who work at the gas station where I always stop, or the other parents whose kids are on the same T-ball team as my daughter. We enjoy the games together and can have polite conversations at the awards picnic.

This group also includes very temporary relationships, such as those developed when negotiating with a merchant, a person providing me service, or a salesperson of some kind. We can develop a temporary relationship based on the understanding that each of us can provide something that the other person needs, wants, or has. Should I find that the other person is deceiving me, I have no reservations about ending the relationship or even telling the person to his face that I believe that he has lied. At the same time, I might have fewer qualms about lying to him. I might think the worst sanction I could suffer, assuming that

With the members of the social group, there is no guarantee that each will be honest with the other.

what I have done is not illegal, would be to have to find someone else to provide me what I wanted; however, the person whom I have victimized with my deceit may try to publicly humiliate or berate me for what I have done.

With the members of this group, there is no guarantee that each will be honest with the other. In some cases it may be expected that some form of deceit will be present and it is the duty of each person to protect himself and take all the appropriate precautions. In general, you will find it a greater challenge to spot deception by a person in this group. Yet at the same time, because of the temporary nature of the contact, this is when you may need to be the most diligent. Placing too much trust in people in this group could have costly consequences. In other words, you wouldn't want to entrust your money to the guy who sits with you in the bleachers at the kids' T-ball game without doing at least the due diligence you would with a stranger.

Public

The final group includes the rest of the world, which we will call the "public" group. This would include politicians, world leaders, sports figures, media or entertainment figures, or other very high-profile people whose actions we are observing from a distance.

The members of this group have a large public platform that they can use to perpetuate their deception. This goes back to the old political saying that you can fool some of the people a lot of the time and a lot of the people some of the time but you can't fool all of the people all of the time. Efforts at deception in this arena are designed to protect the person's public image and ultimately the ability to control a lot of people. Therefore, the goal of the deception is primarily selfish.

We should be very concerned about deceit from members of our public group.

Should a person in the public classification be caught in a deception, he may be charismatic enough to overcome the damage or engage in more deception to diminish the apparent damage from the initial lie. The exposed deceiver also can be confident that in a very short time his transgression will be forgotten by the public as another scandal or crisis takes the headlines. After a few years he may be nearly forgiven for mistakes if, in fact, they are at all vividly remembered for what they really were—an abuse of the public trust.

Members of our public group are most likely individuals with whom we have not had nor ever will have direct contact. In this day and age, we may not even experience outrage for having our trust so callously ignored by these public individuals. We reason that they are so far removed from us that their actions have little or no impact on our personal lives. In reality, we should be very concerned about such transgressions. These individuals have gained their positions of trust and high public status because we have given it to them. Should they betray that trust and abuse the power, and we do not hold them responsible for such transgressions, by our silence we have approved of what they have done. These individuals represent us and are a representation of who we are and what we should consider to be important attributes in leaders. To not speak out against such deceitful behaviors is to say we approve of their duplicity. Why, then, should we expect anything different from those people in our intimate, personal, and social groups and ultimately ourselves?

When a situation arises in which a public figure may be deceiving the population, you will be faced with deciding for yourself whether you believe the person or not, based on what you see and hear in the public record. To the extent that you can, you'll be able to apply the skills you learn from this book to draw your own independent conclusions about the person's veracity.

Misconceptions

Of all the possible reasons that the general population does poorly at spotting deception, one of the contributing factors is that we look for clues to deceit in the wrong places, or, based on folk wisdom or folklore, we think that deception can be revealed in certain behaviors. Many of these misconceptions seem to develop a life of their own, and it is easy to find people who believe without a doubt that these symptoms are totally reliable in their accuracy. Some of the problems associated with a failure at successfully identifying deception have to do with our attitude about our ability. There are plenty of people who put blind faith in the ability always to be able to spot deception, or always to spot deception in a specific person: "Oh, I can *always* tell when he's lying." I know of one person who says that body language tells him all he needs to know and he doesn't really need to pay attention to any other signals.

Over the years of teaching and doing research of the training materials in the criminal justice field, I have been amazed at some of the things I have seen taught as signs of deception. I've also been amused at what some criminal justice students and police officers have told me that they were taught. Some of the symptoms identified were old folk wisdom that I had heard many times while other supposed signs of deception were truly very peculiar and made no sense at all. These kinds of misinformation are confusing and contribute to the dismal job we all do at spotting deceit.

Most of the misconceptions about how to spot deception deal with watching a person's face and eyes and listening for verbal cues. For example, there are those who believe that a truthful person can always look you in the eye, while someone who is lying cannot. Another interesting misconception, which has even invaded the academies of law enforcement, is that you can determine if a person is lying by watching whether he breaks eye contact to the right or the left. Unfortunately there is no scientific evidence to support this idea. In fact, attempts to study this phenomenon have failed to support this belief. There are no reliable signs of deception based solely on the amount of eye contact a person maintains. Of course, this is a difficult misconception to shake, given all the old detective movies where suspects had "shifty eyes."

In addition to the eyes, many people traditionally watch another person's face in hopes of spotting deception. In many cases they don't even know what they are looking for—some unknown symptom or tell-tale clue from the face that will alert them when a person has been deceptive. However, of all the areas of the body, the head and face generate the fewest symptoms. The main reason is that the speaker is consciously or even subconsciously aware of this type of scrutiny and will generally do a good job at suppressing signs of deception from the face.

There are also those who believe that the crossing of arms or legs during a conversation is an undeniable sign of deception. A person who exhibits a fair amount of fidgeting with his hands or who squirms in his chair may be unjustly identified as a liar. Another common misconception has been that someone who says "ah," "er," "uh," or "um" many times in speech is lying.

We look for clues to deceit in the wrong places.

In the upcoming sections dealing with each of the areas of verbal and nonverbal behaviors, we will discuss which symptoms are reliable signs of deception and those that are merely indicators of general stress. It has been my experience that the unreliable techniques for spotting deception have been primarily "gimmicks." Someone may have spotted the behavior once or twice, and it happened to coincide accidentally with a moment during which a person was being deceptive. I hope to eliminate many of those misconceptions by the time you finish reading this book, giving you the full picture of how to reliably spot deception. Your accuracy rate should improve, and with it your communication skills.

GUIDELINES
and basic PRINCIPLES

Chapter Two

A ll human communication uses four very general methods or "channels." We communicate through body language or nonverbal behavior, voice quality, speech content, and through very small, fleeting messages called micro signals or "micro expressions."[1]

Body language (the nonverbal channel) makes up the bulk of human communications, perhaps as much as 65 percent of our output.[2] You also may hear nonverbal behaviors referred to as "kinesic behaviors," which is a term coined by the first serious observer of body language, Professor Ray L. Birdwhitsell, at the University of Louisville in the early 1950s. The other channels—voice quality, speech content, and micro expressions—make up the remaining 35 percent of communication. The purpose of this book is to teach you how to identify behaviors in each of these categories that can help determine the credibility of a person's statements to you.

We all react to our environment and its many stimuli on two levels—the mental (or cognitive) level and the emotional level.

We all react to our environment and its many stimuli on two levels—the mental (or cognitive) level and the emotional level. Our reactions are communicated through the four channels of body language, voice quality, speech content, and micro expressions, all of which are tuned or programmed to act in concert to express our emotional and mental responses. Together they create harmony like that of a string quartet. This "quartet" has practiced all of our individual lives, but deception is much like having one or more members of the quartet playing out of tune. To complicate the issue, one or more of the members is playing a slightly different version of a musical piece and in our role as the conductor we are trying to direct the quartet without any sheet music. You can imagine the unpleasant sounds that are going to be produced. When we are attempting to lie or deceive another we are upsetting the delicate balance of our own communication system and our attempts to control the output can have disastrous results. It is these moments of "communication disharmony" that can create tell-tale signs that a person is under serious emotional and/or mental stress, and may possibly be lying or deceiving in his communication.

Our reactions are communicated through the four channels of body language, voice quality, speech content, and micro expressions.

Part of the complication for us in trying to control our communication output under the duress of deception is our attitude about being deceptive. You will recall that I mentioned that we react to our environment on two levels—cognitive and emotional. I may, to a limited extent, be able to control some of my mental processes when I lie. For example, I may have done something wrong and I'm concerned that my actions may be uncovered. Conversely, I may be trying to sell you something or give you a quote on fixing your roof or car. In anticipation of possible discovery, I try to prepare my statement or "alibi" ahead of time. I try to anticipate every possible question I might be asked just so I'll be fully prepared; however, in reality, I'm never going to be fully prepared. I may be asked questions I never anticipated or asked a question in a form different from that which I expected.

Now I must create a new line of thought on the spur of the moment. I'm going to have to remember my previous deceptive statements and make sure my new responses match previous remarks. At the same time, I'm going to have to remember the deviation in my deception plan so I can keep the lie alive in future responses. All of this is a great deal to ask of a person under stress.

As much as I may try to plan my mental reactions and responses, I have to try to do the same for emotional reactions. Unfortunately, it is far more difficult to plan my emotional reactions ahead of time. No matter how much I think and plan mentally for such a future stressful situation, it is very difficult to anticipate how I am going to feel when that specific moment arrives. To complicate matters even more, I have to control both the emotional and cognitive reactions at the same time and keep them balanced so I can avoid detection. The difficulty of trying to avoid imbalance in behaviors is aggravated by the fact that I may at the same time be worried about one or more additional concerns.

A person may mislead others out of fear of punishment, because he's after some form of reward, or because he is in general fear of the situation itself.

When I do choose to be deceitful, I have some additional concerns about my lie, which are going to occupy my thoughts and influence my behaviors while I deceive. One of the concerns I may have is what might happen if my lie fails. In other words, what is going to happen to me if other people discover I am lying? This takes us back to an issue raised earlier about deception. I may be misleading or misinforming others in the first place because I'm fearful of being punished for my actions, because I'm after some form of reward, or because I am in general fear of the situation itself. On top of those concerns, I'm worried about the consequences of the fact that I have lied and what is going to happen as a result. Do you sense a very complicated scenario developing here? There are entirely too many mental and emotional issues to deal with at one time when a person is lying. This is why a keen observer may be able to identify the signs of deception.

Another possible complication involves the perception of myself as a deceiver. In some cases or with some types of people, deceivers do in fact feel bad about lying to someone else. Their concern about deception generates increasing feelings of guilt. Most people do feel some sense of guilt or remorse when they choose to engage in a lie. These additional feelings of remorse or guilt can contribute signals in the four channels of communication that make it possible to detect a lie.

Some people may actually experience a sense of joy or pleasure while lying. This behavior has been referred to as "duping delight."[3] A person may experience this phenomenon because he sees his deception as part of a game, and he may be winning at this point, particularly if he perceives that the other person appears to be buying into the lie. It may now be difficult for him to maintain control of the emotional elation he feels, just

The seven keys to detecting deception are: constant, change, clusters, consistency, preconceptions, contamination, and cross-checking.

as it is difficult to maintain control over guilty feelings. Again, this surge of emotion can cause him to signal in his body language, voice quality, speech content, or micro expressions that he is lying.

The task of interpreting the truthful and deceptive behaviors of other people can be very challenging for at least a couple of reasons. First, human communication behavior can be very complex and at times very confusing. Second, the ability to diagnose such behaviors with some level of accuracy can be quickly compromised because we have to overcome our own personal biases, misconceptions, and pre-conceptions. If we hope to overcome these stumbling blocks, we must take the appropriate precautions in our analysis efforts to reduce the risk of misinterpreting another person's honesty. Nothing could be worse than wrongly accusing a truthful person of being deceptive, but, of course, you don't want to be lied to either.

To help reduce the chances of making these serious errors, we are going to establish a set of rules to use when we are making our analysis of someone's behavior. These basic rules are critical as we explore the symptoms of deception. There are seven easy-to-remember guidelines that will help you identify the signs that the person you're talking to is under stress in the conversation. These seven guidelines will help you identify those times when you should pay special attention to a conversation and be on the lookout for a lie. It will be up to you to use these guidelines in a way that enhances your communication and relationships.

Constant

Guideline #1: You must identify a person's constant or normal behavior before you can identify any other significant behaviors.

The clues that you are going to use to help you diagnose someone's deceptive behavior are those that indicate a shift or deviation from his constant emotional or mental state. The only way you can identify these critical shifts in the behavior of those around you is to have a fairly good understanding of what constitutes their normal behavior.

For example, over the years I have had to travel quite a lot, sometimes as much as 180 nights per year. Being away from my wife and family has made it all the more important to me to keep the communication open, so I talk to them almost every day. As you might imagine, I have a pretty good memory—you could even describe it as a "feel" for the sound of my wife's voice. In fact, it was over the telephone that we first met. She worked in one state for a government agency and I worked in another.

In any conversation with my wife over the phone, I can tell a lot about how her day has been going just by the quality of her voice. I can tell instantly from the sound of her voice and the rate of her speech if she is tired, or if she is coming down with the flu. Her tone of voice also can tell me if one or both of my daughters is in hot water. And her speech content might include clues like, "Let me tell you what *your* children have done."

The person's constant is the benchmark for your diagnostic process. All of your subsequent analysis of a person's communications, both truthful and deceptive, will be compared to this benchmark. Identifying a constant for the person whom you are observing can be accomplished through several means. If the person you are watching happens to be someone with whom you are already familiar, all you need to do is mentally review your past experiences with that person. Retrace in your mind the times you can recall when the person has been angry, frustrated, under a great deal of stress, in a state of excitement, and other reactive behaviors. What does that person's voice sound like under these conditions? How would you describe the pitch of his voice? Does it change in volume? How much or how little does he gesture using his hands in these situations? When he speaks, are his sentences clear and concise, or does he ramble, stutter, and fail to have complete sentences? What about his facial expressions? Are his expressions exaggerated in appearance or does he become stone-faced? These are the characteristics of a person's behaviors with which you want to be familiar.

The more familiar you are with a person's regular, or baseline, communication patterns, the more effective you will be at interpreting his deception, evasion, or stress.

Suppose the person you're observing is someone unfamiliar to you. Perhaps it is a person whom you have just met or have had limited contact with in the past; how do you establish the constant for this person? First, the question you may want to ask yourself is how much time do you want to dedicate to finding the constant of behavior and what risks are you willing to take if you don't do a thorough job of finding his baseline? If you wish to accurately diagnose someone's credibility and hope to make an informed decision from the information you have obtained, spending some quality time in finding his constant is the first place to begin. It needn't be a long involved task, but you do need to try to engage the person in a conversation about topics that are not of a critical nature or are not connected with the primary issue about which you are concerned. Talk about family, sports, weather, movies, or, better still, engage the person in a conversation about himself. That is bound to be a topic with which he is thoroughly familiar, and you will hopefully put him at ease. Second, you'll get the opportunity to develop some good background information about the person and maybe get a little feel for his personality. It is often quite revealing to listen to a person talk about himself and hear what he thinks is important for others to know. Listening to how he describes his successes, failures, or personal interests tells you what is important to him and can give you some great insights. You also can learn a lot about the person based on how he talks about other people, friends, business associates, and family members. Besides, if you're going to be judging the truthfulness of another person's communications with you, it's best done by lots of listening and observing, and not necessarily by lots of talking.

What if you are interested in deciding whether you think someone in the public eye is lying? Perhaps you are deciding how to cast your vote, or are just interested in his situation. How do you get a constant on someone who moves in the public arena such as politicians, actors, sports figures, businesspeople, or others who are extremely visible to the public through the press? It's obviously going to be hard for you to control the conditions under which you can find the constant of behavior, but the press will give you opportunities to observe interviews, and you don't have to worry about stimulating the person to talk or interact with you because someone else has taken on that role. All you have to do is sit back, watch, listen, and focus your concentration. The more publicly visible the person is or the more often he is covered by the press in a variety of situations, the larger the catalog you will have to rely upon to establish the baseline. Don't rely, however, on staged or scripted events such as commercials, political ads, infomercials, movies, speeches, and so forth. Your assessment will be more accurate if you can observe that person under more spontaneous situations, such as press conferences, when the press is allowed to ask any questions they want. Television newsmagazine shows, investigative news shows, or open-topic talk shows are more likely to give you a more realistic sample to use for identifying a constant for that person. Don't worry if the person has been well groomed to appear in public. A person who is going to be deceptive—even if well-groomed or well-rehearsed—can and frequently will still generate deception cues that you may be able to identify. Remember, nobody can catch all the symptoms and signs of deception at the moment they happen. You just want to be able to catch as many of those symptoms as you can so you can make an accurate and informed decision about the person's credibility.

Change

Guideline #2: Look for a change in the person's constant: a new behavior or an existing behavior that stops or changes significantly.

Once you feel that you have an understanding of a person's baseline, or constant, you can begin to look for changes in a person's behavior constant when trying to identify deception. There are three basic ways in which a person will undergo some form of change caused by the stress associated with deception. Either you will see a new behavior that you have not observed previously, an existing one will stop, or the appearance of an existing behavior will change significantly.

Let's assume that you are evaluating a politician who is holding a press conference regarding the building of a new road in your state. He has been taking questions about the cost, how long it will take, and how many new jobs it will mean for the people of the state. So far, he's been very articulate and has had no trouble expressing himself. Then, a news reporter asks him if, in fact, some of the money for this project has come from the social security surplus, which he had said during his campaign that he would never allow. He responds to the question something like this: "Well, now I uh...I know this is of great concern and that many people think that...But I've always been for the fixed-income voter, you know, protecting the fixed-income person. This project is going to provide...it's been desperately needed for some time and the loss or the use of some of those funds...you know it's in a better position than it was a year and a half ago." You just heard an important change in the congressman's behavior.

One of the training tapes that I use when teaching interview and interrogation courses involves a young man who consistently keeps his hand up around or often even covering his mouth. This young man does this even when he is telling the truth. It is a behavior that for other individuals can be a sign of deception, but this subject does it almost the entire time. Except, of course, when he is responding to a few key questions. For example, he is asked how he and his brother chose the drugstore they burglarized and he answers that they had chosen the drugstore at random. At that moment, he covers his nose and eyes with his hand. In this case, the subject stopped his normal behavior and engaged in a new symptom. Moments later, in response to another question, the young man tells the interviewer that they had been to that town before and had picked out that specific drug store as their target.

Behaviors that are significant will be timely.

You may have a child who gestures frequently when she talks. You might even say that she "talks with her hands." But at the moment when you ask her about a vase that got turned over on the table so that the water stained the wood, you see her hide her hands behind her back as she explains how the cat jumped on the table while chasing a fly and that must be how the vase got turned over. Your daughter has changed her existing communication behavior. Who really knocked over the vase?

These behaviors that you are learning to identify don't just happen out of thin air. Something causes them to happen. There has been some form of stimulus that caused the reaction on the part of the person you are observing. That stimulus can come in the form of a question from you, an observation that person has made, or from an emotion or thought within himself as he considers something he may wish to communicate to you, and so on. The significance of the stimulus itself is what is going to be important to explore. The timing of the person's reaction is going to be anywhere from three to five seconds after that key stimulus. Since the time frame is relatively short, it will be extremely important for you to focus all your attention on this person's verbal and nonverbal behavior nearly all the time. A moment of distraction may cause a failure to recognize that something of importance has just caused the person's behavior to change.

One of the mistakes that is frequently made by observers of deception is classifying deceptive behavior they have seen or heard in response to the wrong question or stimulus. You may have witnessed a deceptive response if you have just seen your employee cover his mouth, lean his body away from you, shrug his shoulders, and answer, "Yes," when you asked him if he sent the contract bid in before the deadline. It does not mean he was lying to you when you asked him two minutes ago about the amount he billed you for overtime. You must limit your analysis to one specific response. You cannot make a broad assessment of all of a person's behaviors just on the basis of a single answer or reaction. What was the specific question you asked just prior to seeing this person's reaction? What was the last stimulus the person experienced just before he gave you his answer? It is the response to that specific issue to which you should limit your analysis.

If you will recall from our discussion in the previous chapter, we all react to the world or environment around us on two primary levels—emotional and mental. We would prefer that the world be orderly and predictable all the time, but obviously we can't control the conditions around us. Through years of practice, we have developed some fairly ingrained habits in our behaviors. For the most part, we will have developed some fairly consistent behaviors when we are happy, sad, frustrated, upset, relaxed, and so forth. In the same vein, we also have spent many years practicing our communications with those around us and have developed a fine balance in our expressions of feelings and ideas. You will recall that we talked about the well-rehearsed quartet of communication channels we use when we express ourselves. We communicate best when all the members of that quartet are playing the same piece of music with the same feeling, at the same tempo, at the correct volume. Then all four parts are blending together nicely. Deception creates disharmony in that quartet and it shows in the performance.

For example, my partner and I were conducting an investigation for one of our clients regarding a sum of money missing from a financial institution. There were only a small number of people who could have had access to the money and would have had any opportunity to take it. Our investigation had narrowed down the possible suspects to two people. The older of the two had hired the younger man to help him repossess a car. The normal procedure was to make contact with the owner of the car face to face and, if at all possible, obtain a payment. If they could not get the payment, one man would drive the repossessed car back to the bank and the other man would drive their personal car back to the bank. In the instance we were investigating, the men were able to obtain back payments and therefore did not repossess the car. The next morning, when the older man returned to the bank with the cash, half of the money was missing.

We began interviewing the older of the two men. We spent some time discussing how the men did their job for the bank. We also learned that they had other jobs that they worked at part time. I discussed in detail the older man's financial condition, asked about any problems with loans, school, doctor's bills, gambling debts, and so

forth. I didn't spot any tale-tell signs. I moved on to the events surrounding the repossession of the car a week earlier, asking the older
man to go through the details of that afternoon step by step. I finally
came to the point where I had to confront the man with the question
of whether he stole the money. Without hesitation he told me, "No." I
asked him if he knew who took the money and he said, "No." I saw
no signs of dishonesty with either answer.
After more conversation, I became really frustrated because I couldn't figure out what I was
missing. In desperation, I finally asked, "Well,
then, what in the world happened to the

Be on the alert for timely and significant changes in a person's verbal or nonverbal behavior.

money? Did you lose it?" Instantly, I saw a dramatic change in the
man's facial expression and I watched his body language change
from upright and erect to slumping in the chair. This change was not
only dramatic, but it also occurred in response to a stimulus—a particular question that I had posed. I had blurted out, "Did you lose it?"
and because I was keenly aware of the dramatic, timely change in
the man's constant, I was able to pursue this line of questioning. The
older man genuinely thought he had lost the money. As it turns out,
the younger man had stolen it from his pocket, which we were able
to discover in a later interview with the younger man.

The reason that changes in a person's constant are indicators of
something going on is because when a person practices deception, he
is forced to consider more than one train of thought and more than
one true emotional response. These multiple levels of response wind
up taxing a person's ability to focus his concentration. Trying to
entertain more than one thought at a time is psychologically impossible, but a good lie, if there is such a thing, demands some mixture
of truth and deception. As we said before, the larger the lie, the
greater the challenge to remember all of its integral parts. We must
concern ourselves with previous lies in order to make sure that the
follow-up deception correctly matches and leaves the new lie open
enough to be able to add onto if necessary. Besides being challenged

at creating and sustaining the deception, we must be able to keep our emotional responses in check and ensure that they are synchronized with our verbal output. This is quite a lot to accomplish all at one time and we frequently fail to do so. What results are the symptoms of deception we generate during our responses.

This imbalance between thoughts and emotions can create a significant change in behavior, and it is this change that you can hope to spot and identify while decoding another person's communications. Therefore, it is the change from a person's constant of behavior that highlights the area most likely to hold deception.

Clusters

Guideline #3: Human communication is a complex interaction of many verbal and nonverbal behaviors, each of which is a response to internal and external stimuli.

If we were able to identify just one single behavior that proved someone was being either truthful or deceptive, people would rarely get away with lying to each other. Unfortunately, however, that is not the case. As much as we would like to be able to identify single significant behaviors, human communication is just far too complex. An element that contributes to the complexity is the fact that we all have our own individual menu of behaviors we use anytime we are communicating with someone else. These behaviors are stimulated by the different emotions we may be experiencing at any particular moment. The types of gestures we use may change from time to time, depending on the intimate, personal, social, or public classification of the person with whom we are interacting. We also rely on gestures and cues that are part of a habitual pattern of response we may use when expressing a particular set of ideas. Someone else in the same situation or even the same setting may use an entirely different set of interaction behaviors and

A cluster of behaviors is more significant than a single, random behavior.

gestures and a different set of emotional expressions that are also unique to him. We cannot assume, therefore, that there are one-size-fits-all gestures that are applicable to all people.

Here is an example: you notice a person sitting near a departure gate at an airport. Upon close examination, you notice that he appears to be crying. Now, what are all the possible reasons that this man could be crying? Perhaps he is going to be flying to another city to the funeral of a recently deceased family member and he is grieving over the loss of that family member. Perhaps his son has just gotten on a plane and is flying to a military base and preparing to go into a dangerous military situation on the other side of the world and he fears for his son's life. But wait, people cry for other reasons, too. His daughter and son-in-law are returning from being overseas for two years and he is about see his granddaughter for the first time and he is crying tears of joy. His wife is returning from a long treatment at a medical facility on the other side of the country and she has been cured. Hold on now. They have been laying new carpet in the airport and the smell of carpet glue is really strong. Maybe he is allergic to the smell of the glue. He could have just had cataract surgery and the bright sunlight is painful to his now-sensitive eyes. All the above could be reasonable explanations for why you might see a man crying while sitting in the waiting area of the airport.

With these examples in mind, consider the mistakes that could be made when trying to judge another person's honesty based on a single cue. Just as with the unique gestures I use when I'm interacting with another person, I have a similar personal menu of signals I may exhibit when I'm deceitful. What I may exhibit as deception cues are symptoms that you may never use or only use infrequently. If you believe that a particular nonverbal cue is a sure sign of deception, you may spend our entire conversation watching to see if I exhibit that one specific cue, which I may never use. In the meantime, you could miss a significant number of other nonverbal and verbal cues that I've been lying to you all along.

Let's consider another complication that may occur. Suppose you have identified a symptom that you believe is generally reliable for helping you identify dishonesty. At some point during our conversation, you notice that I appear to have exhibited that one suspicious signal. The question now will be, was that just an accidental behavior or was it really significant? Some behaviors appear to happen accidentally. They can occur at random and have nothing to do with an attempt to deceive the listener. You have now

The burden of proof is squarely on the ability of the observer to spot deception and not on the speaker to prove that he is being truthful.

misidentified a truthful person as being deceptive. What happens to your credibility at being able to spot deception? What kind of damage have you just done to the relationship you had with this person? What kind of faith are you going to have in your ability to spot deception from someone in the future when it may be very important to be able to do so? Avoid the pitfall of making a diagnosis of a person's honesty on the basis of a single behavior because there is no single behavior, verbal or nonverbal, that proves that a person is being truthful or deceptive.

Think about this first basic guideline on a more practical level. A police officer on the interstate pulls over a driver whom he suspects of being intoxicated while driving. The officer does not come to the conclusion that the driver is impaired until he has conducted several reliable field sobriety tests—touching the nose, counting backwards, reciting the alphabet, and walking a straight line, to name a few. Only after observing the driver while performing these tasks does the officer draw a conclusion about the driver's sobriety or impairment. The officer would certainly be remiss should he testify that the driver must have been impaired merely because he was driving slowly or swerved once while on the road.

In your observations of verbal and nonverbal behavior, you should not make a decision on the truthfulness of a person's statements based solely on a single behavior. Human behavior is far too complex and the behaviors that people exhibit during communication can be very individualized. What applies to one person may not apply at all to another, yet there may be some symptoms that two or more individuals share. Nothing in human behavior is absolute or exact. Later we will discuss the significance of individual behaviors and identify those that most often occur when a person is more likely to be deceptive. None of these behaviors is totally foolproof in identifying deception and the apparent absence of symptoms does not necessarily indicate that a person is being truthful. There will be times when even a truthful person may randomly generate symptoms that can appear to indicate deceit but are merely accidental phenomenon or have been misidentified by the observer. The odds, however, that two, three, or even more symptoms occurring at one moment are a random occurrence is possible but very unlikely.

We can use the previous example of the police officer stopping a driver to illustrate the importance of clusters. We have already established that the officer would not come to the conclusion that the driver is driving while intoxicated solely because the driver was weaving on the road or merely driving more slowly than the posted speed limit. Should the officer attempt to testify in court that he had concluded that the driver was impaired based on those two very limited symptoms, there is no doubt that the case would be thrown out of court. Instead, the officer must look for a cluster of indications the driver had been consuming alcohol. Slurred speech, the smell of alcohol on the driver's breath, beer cans or an open liquor bottle on the floorboard of the car,

In your observations of verbal and nonverbal behavior, you should not make a decision on the truthfulness of a person's statements based solely on a single behavior.

the driver appearing unstable on his feet, and the driver being unable to walk a straight line when requested to do so, taken together in some combination, would be what the officer needed to cite the driver. The officer may further observe that the driver was unaware of what town he was in and what day of the week it was.

The officer may also tell the judge that the driver was operating the car without any headlights at 3 A.M., was doing 75 miles per hour in a 55 miles per hour zone, and was going eastbound in the westbound lane. On top of that, when the driver submitted to a breathalyzer test, it indicated that the person had a blood alcohol level of .32 when the legal intoxication limit for that state is .10. All of these factors considered together lead the officer to believe that the driver was driving while under the influence. Our definition of a cluster is very similar. A single symptom by itself is not sufficient evidence to come to the conclusion that the person is being deceptive, but multiple symptoms occurring at one moment when discussing a single issue can indicate a strong possibility of deception.

Consistency

Guideline #4: A consistent reaction to a specific issue can be a significant indicator of deception.

We indicated earlier that the way for an observer to spot deception is to look for changes in a person's normal or constant of behavior. As we will learn later on, not all the changes that you see are indications that someone is lying to you, but he merely can be acting under a function of general stress. The deception-oriented changes that I generate occur because there is conflict between the emotions I really feel and the emotions that I intend you to see. Those changes you see happen because of the conflict I experience trying to keep all those emotional issues in check. Until I can become accustomed to and control the projected messages and come to terms with my true internal messages, there is always going to be some consistent form of negative reaction from me when you ask me to address that particular topic. I won't have the same problem with any other insignificant issue.

You already know that there is no single behavior that proves a person is being truthful or deceptive and that you must try to identify behaviors in clusters. If the issue under discussion is really of significance to the speaker and the speaker must continue to protect his deception, you should keep getting some form of reaction each time you raise that topic. This is not to suggest, however, that the person will exhibit exactly the same set of behaviors or cluster every time the point is raised. What you are looking for is some form of cluster that consistently occurs when the topic is being discussed. You want to eliminate the possibility that the behaviors you are observing are random in nature.

One of the keys discovered in research is that for a period of time, a deceptive subject tends to keep reacting to the hot topic or issue. Knowing that a deceptive person is more likely to keep presenting some form of stress or deception cues allows you more or less to test the person about other related topic areas. If you get some form of negative response in only one specific area, you'll know that that is most likely where the deception may be found. After a period of time, however, the intensity of the person's reactions to this suspicious area may diminish. Discussing the topic then will not create the same level of reaction in the person that it did before.

For example, let's say you are a human resources manager and your job is to interview and hire qualified candidates for your company. Perhaps the job vacancy you are trying to fill requires some experience, training, a degree, or other credential. As you are interviewing the applicant and reviewing his employment application, you ask about his degree or specific experiences at a previous job. Whenever this issue is raised, the person becomes evasive or begins stalling with his answers and possibly shows you some significant changes in his body language. This could well be a significant cluster of behaviors suggesting that the person is withholding something about his background. He may never have finished the degree program or may have inflated his skills or experience in a previous job.

You are not looking for the same changes every time, just that there are changes every time and that they arise in clusters.

This is an area you need to explore in greater detail to determine why the person is responding with such remarkable changes in behavior.

What if you were considering hiring a baby-sitter for your kids, or perhaps asking questions of someone who was to be a house-sitter while you were away on an extended vacation? Wouldn't you like to know for sure if that sitter was a responsible person and could be trusted with your home or children? Significant changes in his demeanor can be telling you to be more inquisitive about that person's background. Consistent reactions by the person during the discussions of particular issues should be a signal for you to continue to probe for more accurate details. You will want to keep coming back to the question or issue that seems to evoke a cluster of changes to the person's constant and see if that happens every time you get close to that topic in your conversation. Remember, you're not looking for the same changes every time, just that there are changes every time and that they arise in clusters. When you notice that this is happening, you will want to prolong the conversation, moving away from the key issue, then circling back to it and observing closely what happens.

Preconceptions

Guideline #5: To use your skills to the fullest, approach conversations with an open mind; observations based on preconceptions or misconceptions are not reliable.

From the very beginning of this book, I have tried to make the point that in general people do a very poor job of determining if they have been or are going to be the victims of deception by another person. I also have tried to point out to you why we do such a bad job at identifying deception. Some of the causes for our failures have been attributed to identifying the wrong behaviors as reliable signs of deceit. I have warned you about the risk of trying to identify deception on the basis of single behaviors, because there is no single behavior that reliably indicates truth or deception for all people. Compounding the pitfalls of misconceptions are personal prejudices or preconceptions.

The accuracy of your analysis of another person's truthfulness rests on your ability to put aside any preconceived notions you may have about whether the person is going to be truthful or deceptive. If you make your observations with the assumption that this person is probably going to lie to you, then all you are going to see are those symptoms that confirm your suspicions, whether the person is exhibiting true symptoms of deception or not. Human beings are notorious for frequently deciding on the solution and then creating an argument that will support the conclusions that they have made already.

For example, I have this belief about the driving abilities of the residents of a certain state. I believe that they must be the worst, most reckless, and dangerous drivers in the entire United States. Not just some of the drivers from this place, but every last one of these people is a rotten driver. I hate to share the road with them!

First of all, they always drive over the speed limit. They're all crazy! In the fast lane, they just fly by you. But if I ever need to pass another car and pull into the passing lane, they slow down to match the speed of the car I am trying to pass. They show no concern for the fact that traffic is piling up behind them. Also, these people are notorious for tailgating or even flashing their lights to get me to pull over. Whenever I see a particularly terrible driver, I don't need to see his license plate to know what state he's from!

Does it sound as though I have a case of road rage? What's feeding my negative opinion about these drivers? My preconceptions are selecting my observations—I'm keenly on the lookout for instances that confirm my suspicions and expectations. However, my observations tell only half of the story. It is improbable that every single person in that state is a terrible driver, but by seeing only what I want to see—examples that reinforce my preconception—it certainly appears that way. My preconceptions have weakened my observation skills and I have made a faulty judgment. When you are trying to determine if someone is lying to you, and relationships are at stake, you want to be careful to avoid preconceptions and remain objective.

Can you think of anything worse than to be telling the truth and, no matter what you say, not be believed? What must that be like for the spouse or teenager whom you have accused of deception but who is actually being truthful? Think how dysfunctional a relationship can become if it is built more on suspicion than on mutual respect or trust. The person who should be so important in your life is less likely to confide in you, share hopes and dreams with you, or even come to you for advice and support if he feels as though he must continually defend himself when speaking with you.

Conversely, preconceptions can cut the other way and make you vulnerable to deception. If you cannot believe that the good looking guy you met at the company picnic would be anything less than truthful, you are setting yourself up to become the victim of another person's deception because you will never see the lies coming. This is not to say that you should believe all the gossip you hear about someone. In fact, if you are using your new deception detecting skills, you should be able to figure out when someone is embellishing a story. At the same time, though, are you ignoring some obvious warning signs of deceit because you just don't want the rumors to be true? Do you believe his lies because to do otherwise would mean that the others were correct in warning you about this dishonest fellow? If you convince yourself that they are lying, then you will end up convincing yourself that the handsome liar is being honest. This is not to say that you should be so paranoid as to believe that everyone is going to lie to you. Hopefully, you are also not so naïve as to believe that everyone tells the truth. You can, however, learn to do a better job at correctly decoding the way other people communicate with you and be more aware of how you communicate with them.

Your next question at this point might be, "How do I avoid the dangers of preconceptions?" Before you made an assessment about this person's honesty, did you identify his constant of behavior? Can you identify possible deception based on the existence of clusters and not on single behaviors? Does he consistently show clusters of signs of deception when you discuss specific issues with him? Have you identified the changes that you have seen that are reliable signs of deception? We are going to examine this issue in greater detail when we discuss cross-checking a little later.

Contamination

Guideline #6: You are a stimulus, and some of your behaviors can affect the behaviors and reactions of the other person in a way that contaminates the accuracy of your observations.

I mentioned earlier that those behaviors that are important to you as the observer are those behaviors that are timely. In discussing that rule, I indicated that the person with whom you are interacting is going to be reacting to the most recent stimulus he experienced. Your goal is to determine the reason for this person's response to that stimulus. Remember that you are the source of the stimulus, and as such, how you are behaving has an impact on the situation you are observing.

You may feel that you are incapable of such sustained attention to the smallest detail involving your attitude and the "vibes" you are giving off, in addition to the contamination caused by the environment. So, here are a few conditions that can make such concentration a little easier to accomplish. First, if you are having a conversation, either with someone close to you or with a stranger, in which you want to be on the alert for lying, try to have that conversation when you are not in a hurry, and in a location that will be free of distractions. Even if you are feeling anxious and as though a great deal is at stake, try to remain relaxed and at ease with yourself. Don't try to interview a nanny candidate at your office with phones ringing and the fear that your boss will interrupt you at any moment. Similarly, don't try to confront your teenager about money missing from your wallet or purse when you have to leave for a dental appointment in fifteen minutes, when your extended family is about to arrive, or your favorite television show is playing. Arrange to have these conversations in a quiet place, and do everything you can to suffuse the atmosphere with a calm and relaxed attitude. If you are undistracted, and you have plenty of time, you will do a much better job of observing and analyzing the communication that takes place.

During any conversation, you need to remember that the other person is going to be reading and diagnosing your behaviors just as you're reading his. If I have a longstanding relationship with the person whom I am now observing, he also should have developed a pretty good understanding of my constant of behavior. The person may be responding to me in a manner based on our past communications and relationship, and whether that past history has been good or bad will be reflected in his reactions to me. The question you need to ask yourself is whether or not he is reacting to the way you are behaving, rather than to the topic of the conversation. There can be times when our actions and reactions are far stronger and more important to the other person than the topic of discussion.

The behaviors I see from another person may be the result of what he is seeing in my behavior. If I am aggressive, condescending, or disinterested, the response of the person with whom I am communicating may very well be a reflection of my behavior and communication. The following story is a perfect example of contamination.

A few years ago, I bought a bottle of expensive perfume for my wife. She had sampled the fragrance during a recent visit to one of our larger local department stores. As a surprise and for no particular reason, I bought her the perfume as a gift. It was a great opportunity for me to express my affection for her by giving her an expensive gift she really wanted.

Not too many months after receiving her gift, my wife noticed that the bottle was about half empty. This is perfume and you don't splash it on like men's aftershave. It was apparent to her that someone had been in her perfume and had wasted a large amount of it. She soon noticed that one of our cats exuded a strong odor of perfume. My wife immediately launched a major investigation to determine which person had committed this terrible crime. I was out of town so I was immediately cleared as a suspect in the case. My wife had not wasted her own perfume on the cat, therefore there were only two other possible suspects—our daughters.

My wife confronted both daughters regarding the case of the missing perfume. Each child adamantly denied any knowledge of the incident. My wife insisted that one of the two was lying to her. Highly agitated and making no progress at finding out the truth, my wife announced that if someone didn't confess to the crime, both girls would receive severe punishment for lying to their mother and that way she would at least get the guilty party. In short order, my younger daughter confessed to the crime. She was sentenced to two weeks in her room with no television and the suspension of other privileges.

A few days after the "investigation," my older daughter made a comment and my wife suddenly realized that the wrong child had been convicted and punished for the crime. She immediately confronted my older daughter, who confessed to having sprayed the poor cat. My wife then asked the younger child why she had confessed to the crime, to which she responded, "Getting grounded is a lot better than getting a spanking!" Astonished at the turn of events, my wife asked the older child why she would allow her little sister to be punished for something that she in fact had done. She responded, "Well, if she's stupid enough to confess to doing it, that's her fault."

My daughters' reactions were not to the question of who was ultimately responsible for wasting the perfume, but to the threat that, innocent or not, they might both suffer dire punishment. To my youngest daughter the choice was clear. Their reactions had been "contaminated" by the interviewer's approach to finding the truth.

Cross-Checking

Guideline #7: Before drawing any conclusions, it is necessary to review your observations and cross-check the data.

You are now aware of the pitfalls and perils that can result in erroneously judging the honesty of another person's remarks. I have outlined for you some very important rules and principles that are designed to reduce the risks of making such judgmental errors. The final decision regarding whether you are going to believe this person or not is up to you. You have to have confidence in your ability to identify reliable signs of deception and incriminating behavior. We are going to explore those behaviors that, when researched in detail, have been found to be reliable in isolating deception. It is your duty, however, to be sure that you have made a valid assessment.

A few years ago, I was contacted through a state police agency by the father of a missing teenage girl. She had been missing for about three years. The distraught father had tried everything to find his daughter, including hiring private detectives and psychics. A young man in prison for murder who claimed to know about the girl had recently contacted him. Desperate for information, the man asked the state police to help him and he was referred to me.

With some of the basic facts surrounding the girl's disappearance, I spent two days in prison conducting extensive interviews of the young man. The young man seemed to have a few bits and pieces of general information that sounded legitimate and he could describe the missing girl in detail. He told me about seeing the girl several times and at one point had helped nurse her back to health after she had been injured. I was told about the area of the country where she had been hidden by her captors. If I could get him out of prison he would take me to her.

The father was in total despair and I felt great compassion for him. He wanted the state police to get the young man released so he could take us to find his daughter. However, I was not at all confident that the young man was telling the truth. On some issues I asked him about he was very specific, but when I pushed hard for the details about the girl, her location, her physical condition, and who was holding her, I got evasion and signs of deception. I recommended that the young man not be trusted and that he was lying about his knowledge of the girl, but the father and some of the other people involved in the case were convinced he was telling the truth. I was alone in my belief that the man was lying.

I worried about my analysis of the man's behaviors. Had I missed something? I had spent two days interviewing him face to face. I had also talked to him twice by telephone. I was sure I had a good grasp of his constant of behavior. At times, we had talked about insignificant topics so I could read his baseline. I ran through the areas in which I thought that he was lying and I could identify his deceptive cues that were always in clusters. He always seemed evasive around having seen her, treated her injuries, knowing where she was, and who was holding her. His reactions were consistent and timely.

Did I have any preconceptions? Why was it I didn't trust him? Was it because he was in prison? I really wanted to help this man find his daughter but I couldn't just tell him what he wanted to hear. I had cross-checked thoroughly and had confidence in my analysis.

A few months later, a television program planned to broadcast the story. Everyone involved in the search for the girl, including the man in prison, was interviewed. I was the only person who had no faith in the young man or his story. I could tell that everyone else was not pleased with my conclusions. A week before the television crew was to start filming for the show, the girl was found by police on the other side of the country. She told investigators that she had run away from home three years earlier. She indicated that she had never been injured, did not know a young man in prison, and had never been in the part of the country he had described.

That same week, I learned that the young man had plotted the entire scheme. He planned to make good his escape while ostensibly searching for the girl. He had in fact been in that area of the country and knew it well. He had found a missing person poster about the teenager, had memorized information about her, and gleaned the rest of the details from her unwitting father.

My analysis had turned out to be correct but I had to be sure. Too much was at stake to make a mistake. I had to cross-check my analysis to be sure that I had followed all of my own rules. There had been a lot of pressure on me to ignore my conclusions.

Before coming to a conclusion about whether a person is being truthful or deceptive, you always must ask yourself critical questions about what you observed during your conversation. If you are having doubts about the honesty of the information you're getting in a conversation, it may help you to defer making a decision about the issue

Be fairly strict with yourself when analyzing your conclusions. You do not want to be sloppy when there are relationships at stake.

at hand during that conversation. You may want to ask for time to think about it or arrange to continue the conversation at a later date. After the conversation is over, sit down immediately and make some notes about what was said and what you observed. First, did you establish a constant for that person? Have you known or observed that person for a sufficient period of time in a non-stressful setting that would enable you to fully understand his normal, or non-stressed behaviors? Did you spend time talking about non-stressful issues or discussing topics that should not generate stress or a need to deceive on the part of the person being observed?

Second, can you name the timely, consistent changes that you observed in clusters? Accurately identifying deception should not be based on a "feeling," but on specific behavioral observations. These behaviors were caused by some form of stimulus and each time the topic or issue that created the response was raised, some form of reaction from the person should have been observed. Those behaviors should also be a change from the person's constant pattern of behavior and should occur as a cluster of symptoms. If you can specifically identify when the symptoms occurred, name those specific behaviors accurately, and you have observed them occurring in clusters, then your analysis should be reasonably accurate.

Third, were there any behaviors or actions on your part that may have contaminated this person's behaviors, or are you harboring any preconceptions that could cloud your conclusions? Don't forget that people are watching us at the same time that we are watching them, and having an opinion formed before you make your observations can cause fatal flaws in your analysis of truth and deception. Nothing is more destructive to the relationship between two people than a lack of trust when there is no reason for there to be mistrust.

Fourth, could this be a situation in which a truthful person may be fearful that that you will not believe him? Are you being suspicious for no reason? Is the issue at hand important enough to you to risk damaging the relationship by not believing the other person? Are there other people with whom you can verify the information you are being given? Naturally, in the case of anyone whom you will be hiring or from whom you will be purchasing something, you will want to check references or talk to other satisfied customers.

Finally, could this be a situation in which you may be believing the liar's lie? Strange as it may sound, there are times when believing a lie is far more acceptable than hearing the truth. You may not want to believe that this person could lie to you. You may find the truth upsetting, unsettling, disappointing, or possibly extremely disturbing. The true test is not that you have uncovered the truth, but can you live with it or should you? Again, you must decide how important the matter at hand is to you and your life. If you aren't sure, and the matter is not a serious one, then my advice is always to give another person the benefit of the doubt. You may find that your relationships go more smoothly if you do. So be prepared to carefully cross-check your findings, and be prepared to be fairly strict with yourself in analyzing your conclusions. You will not want to be sloppy when there are relationships at stake. You must honestly question yourself about your motives in trying to decide if this person is being honest. Mentally review each step in your analysis process to determine if you have overlooked anything. Once you have indicated to another person that you believe he is not being honest with you, it may be difficult to take back such an accusation without at least doing some harm to the relationship. If you must make a mistake, err in favor of the other person being honest. You can still minimize your risk of being victimized by proceeding with caution or making further inquiries at a later time.

Verbal
COMMUNICATION

O f all the signals and messages that we "broadcast" when we communicate with someone, the voice only provides about 20 percent of the total output. That 20 percent, however, is very concentrated with information. Because the voice channels are so concentrated, and we are aware that the listener focuses attention on our speech, we work hard at controlling signals we generate with our speech. We have all heard the old folk wisdom, "Weigh your words before you speak," or the more updated version, "Engage brain before putting mouth in gear." I am the first person to hear what I am going to say, and I am aware that the person who is listening to my verbal messages is going to be carefully analyzing my remarks. The same is

Verbal symptoms, one for one, are usually the most productive for identifying stress and deception.

true for everyone. As a result, we are constantly editing our remarks and making very quick assessments about how the message is going to be received and interpreted by the listener. If the message is one filled with deceit, it must be broadcast in such a way that the receiver believes and does not detect the deception. At the same time, we try to control any verbal symptoms that we are under stress because of concern about the deception being detected. As a result of this extensive monitoring of our speech efforts, people are able to generate relatively few verbal symptoms of deceit.

You may be thinking at this point that editing our speech and preparing what we are going to say is a whole lot to worry about, and you would be right. In this section on verbal behavior, we are going to describe what happens when we fail to control all those verbal signs of stress

There are three categories of verbal behavior: voice quality, voice clarity, and speech content.

and signals of deception. With all this effort at controlling our speech we don't generate many verbal deception signals, but when they do occur they are extremely important.

We are going to study verbal behaviors by breaking them down into three categories: voice quality, the clarity of the voice, and the speech content. Understanding how these characteristics work independently and jointly, we can gain insight into the emotional and cognitive behaviors of the person we are observing.

Voice Quality

The quality of the voice is made up of three characteristics: the pitch, the volume, and the rate of speech. Stress or anxiety generally causes a change in at least one of the three attributes of voice quality. In general, these symptoms do not indicate that a person is being deceptive, only that the person is under stress. The changes in voice quality will tell you the person is undergoing a great deal of emotional change, which emotional response the person is experiencing, and how strong that response happens to be.

A key element we have to remember about our speech in general is that when a person speaks, it is because of an internal reaction to some form of external stimulus. There always is some reason that a person chooses to speak. The person, for whatever reason, has identified a mental and/or emotional link between himself and the issue.

The words that are spoken (the content) reveal how the person is dealing with or wants to address the particular issue on a cognitive or mental level. At times and to a lesser degree, the words also may reveal the emotional impact that the issue is having on the person. In other words, voice quality can tell you the type and level of mental response and also sometimes the emotional response being experienced by the speaker.

Changes in voice quality indicate only that the person is under stress.

Pitch

A change from the established constant level of the person's voice provides evidence of the strength of the person's response and the positive or negative characteristics of the response. For example, raised pitch indicates strong internal reactions such as those that are experienced during excitement or when a person is angry or frustrated. A raised pitch also occurs when the person needs to call attention to himself. For whatever reason, he needs to be recognized and have others heed his remarks. A drop in the pitch of the voice suggests the person feels or needs to achieve some form of withdrawal from the issue, such as the emotions experienced in depression or when a person wishes to outwardly play down how important an issue really is to him.

You can see an example of the extremes in voice quality in the character Barney Fife from the classic television sitcom *The Andy Griffith Show*. You could tell when Barney was upset by listening to his squeaky voice. The same tone was apparent when Barney wanted all of Mayberry to pay attention to him and give him his due as deputy sheriff. As another example, think of the voice of a sports announcer calling the game when the score is close and the home team has just made a great play. For an example at the other end of the spectrum, pay attention to the voice of the evening newscaster when he is reporting on the devastation of some natural disaster or the death of a public figure.

Volume

A change in the volume of a person's voice is an excellent indicator of the internal energy level the person feels while communicating. A loud voice is usually associated with excitement, fear, or anger. As it relates to deception, a raised voice may indicate the anger response, which we will be discussing later, or it may indicate a growing level of frustration in a truthful person who feels he is being disbelieved. If the person you are talking to is raising his voice, you want to make sure you are not contaminating the conversation.

A voice volume that drops is most frequently associated with a person who is trying to minimize the focus on a particular topic. Voice volume also may drop when a person is experiencing sadness or depression. A lower volume can be a sign of withdrawal. Have you ever asked your child how things are going in school, or whether his homework is finished, or if he has been studying for that big biology exam? Among other characteristics, have you noticed if his voice volume drops and he begins to answer softly or maybe even to mumble? It may be time to dig a little deeper and find out what is really going on with school! Suppose you've asked your boss if she has made a decision about who is supposed to get the new job. A soft, withdrawn voice may suggest that disappointing news may be on the way for you, that the boss has not yet found the way to tell you you didn't get the position. Suppose you want to discuss a personal issue with someone you consider a friend and you really need his advice. A soft and withdrawn demeanor of the voice along with other verbal and nonverbal cues may indicate that he may not be comfortable discussing this issue with you or may in fact not even find the issue important enough to talk about right now.

> **A person is able to control better his verbal behavior than his body language.**

Speech Rate

The change in a person's speech rate can give us not only some insight into the emotional status of the person but also a glimpse at some of the cognitive processes that may be going on. Rate of speech, or speech rate, is the number of words spoken over a period of time. More simply, how fast is the person talking? A marked increase in words per minute can suggest that the person is angry or excited. A decrease in the speech rate suggests the presence of sadness, disinterest, or difficulty in communicating on this particular topic.

For example, listen to a child who is excited to tell you about what Santa Claus is going to bring for Christmas. Notice the rate of speech of the person who is talking about the new car he won during a radio contest or on a game show. On the other hand, listen to how a friend, a family member, or perhaps a minister delivers bad news to someone. There is a marked change in the rate of speech when a person delivers an uncomfortable or upsetting message to another person.

The rate of speech also will change with the cognitive reaction of the person speaking. It is not unusual for a person's words per minute to increase when delivering a message that has been practiced or rehearsed prior to delivery. Think of the teenager who has gotten a new scratch or dent on the family car while out on a Saturday night. The teenage driver may rehearse that story several times before finally getting home and having to explain the damage to Mom or Dad. The story may not be a lie, but you can bet that the teenager is going to put the best possible spin on it.

When a person's rate of speech decreases significantly from his constant or normal rate, you are witnessing a person who is very carefully measuring his words. This person may have been caught off-guard by the question he has been asked and does not have a prepared line of thought. He now feels he must be very careful with his responses.

Let's stop a moment and take stock of what we have said about the quality changes that occur in the voice. The pitch, that is volume, of the voice may rise or fall, and the rate of speech may change, that is, the person may begin to speak more rapidly or more slowly.

Remember that none of these symptoms by itself indicates that the person is being deceptive, or even truthful for that matter. These changes only tell you that there has been a change in the person's emotional reaction to the issue at hand. You will want to handle the situation accordingly and deal with this person on a particular issue based on his emotional response.

If I intend to use these symptoms to help me assess whether this person is being truthful or deceptive, I need to compare the various aspects of voice quality with other verbal and nonverbal symptoms. When those symptoms are considered together and they disagree with each other or demonstrate conflicting or contradictory messages, then there is a good possibility that the person is not being truthful about his genuine feelings or the message that he is broadcasting. Let's use Barney Fife again as an example. Barney is telling Andy, "I'm not upset." At the same time Barney is saying this, his voice

People who are being deceptive have far more speech dysfunctions than people who are being truthful.

pitch is high and squeaky, he's almost yelling, and he is talking very fast. His verbal cues are in direct contradiction to the content of his speech, and it is obvious that Barney is very upset. Whenever you notice a change in a person's voice quality and the whenever the content of his speech contradicts his voice quality, you will want to watch carefully for deception.

Voice Clarity

It is a psychological impossibility to have more than one thought in your mind at one time. With this concept in mind, think about all the things that a person has to remember if he is going to tell a lie and not get caught. First, he has to remember what the real truth is. Second, he has to remember any previous lies he has already told. Third, he has to figure out a way to match the new lie with the previous lies. And finally, he has to make the new lie easy enough to remember in case he has to lie some more further down the road. Now at the same time he is doing all this mental work, he has to do it under the stress of the moment, as well as being concerned about controlling any verbal and nonverbal signals that may give away the fact that he is being deceptive. That's a lot to juggle mentally for anyone. Failure to successfully handle all these mental activities is frequently revealed in the clarity of the final verbal messages. These verbal mistakes or accidents are collectively referred to as "speech dysfunctions."

Speech Dysfunctions

People who are being deceptive have far more speech dysfunctions than people who are being truthful. As with all the various signs and symptoms we've been discussing, not all cases of speech dysfunction indicate that a person is being deceptive. Some of the mistakes are merely the result of the person experiencing some form of mental stress. However, the presence of the symptoms of speech dysfunction can indicate that the person may be considering that particular moment as an opportunity for deception. Therefore, even though not all the symptoms we are going to discuss mean the person is lying to you, it should still alert you to the fact that you should listen to the person's communications very carefully. While you are diagnosing the clarity of the person's speech, you will need to consider any other verbal and nonverbal symptoms the person may be generating at the same time. Remember, you are looking for clusters of behaviors and not single symptoms.

Stuttering, Stammering, and Mumbling

Most of the forms of speech dysfunction are symptoms with which we are generally familiar. These include symptoms such as stuttering, stammering, or mumbling. The stuttering and stammering symptoms we are talking about are not those that are associated with speech pathology or speech disorders. Prior to the moments when stuttering or stammering occur or become very obvious, the subject has not previously exhibited similar behaviors or does not exhibit them constantly throughout his conversations. Stuttering symptoms occur because the subject may be trying to talk too quickly, while stammering occurs because the subject is trying speak prior to having fully decided or edited what he is trying to say. Mumbling or slurred speech also

"Um," "ah," "er," and other common sounds are not by themselves reliable indicators of deception.

can occur at those moments that the subject has not fully prepared his thoughts before expressing them verbally. The subject is trying to delay his response until his thoughts are in order. Again, these behaviors are more commonly associated with a person who is just experiencing stress and not necessarily trying to lie or engage in deception.

Pausing

Pausing behavior during speech can be very significant to the listener. Pausing can indicate that the speaker has not fully prepared his responses and allows him the time necessary to fully develop his comments. Some observers have found that deceptive subjects tend to have longer delays between the end of a question and the start of their deceptive answers. Those same observers also have found that a person who is being deceptive has far more occurrences of delays within the body of his answers. Unfortunately, this may be a difficult phenomenon to accurately diagnose because of the subjectivity of our perception of what long and short pauses may be. Once again, we must also consider the normal or constant pattern of the speaker when we believe the person is not under stress or is being truthful. The safest assumption you can make about increased pauses during someone's response is that he is possibly considering the option of being deceptive or at least is being evasive or elusive in his responses. You will want to pay special attention to these areas and look for additional confirmation of your analysis of that person's credibility.

Common Sounds

There are some speech sounds that we frequently associate with deception but, in fact, they are not reliable indicators of deception. Among the most common of those sounds are the simple and meaningless stalling tactics—the "ahs," "ers," "ums," and "uhs" that pepper a person's speech. These are most likely nothing more than time-buying efforts on the part of the person to allow him the opportunity to get his thoughts together. Individuals who do not have strong verbal skills seem to have more of these sounds in their speech than those who are generally good at speaking quickly and spontaneously.

Nervous Laughter

The nervous laugh is one of the more interesting speech behaviors that a person may use when he is experiencing stress. First of all, nervous laughter both relieves stress and appears to mask how much anxiety we are really feeling. For example, watch young teenagers during their "courtship ritual" with someone of the opposite sex. Remember when you were that giggling teenager? Nervous laughter serves essentially the same function as whistling or talking to yourself while walking through a graveyard or dark alley. The whistling has a calming effect when a person is scared, and nervous laughter does the same for a person in an uncomfortable situation.

Nervous laughing also can serve as a way to buy time before speaking. It gives the subject that little bit of extra time to think and prepare a safe answer. It is not surprising to find a person that will start to laugh or giggle before speaking as a way to stall their response in a conversation. For example, the person may laugh before answering a question that has been directed toward him. At the same time, the nervous laugh can be a disarming behavior when the situation has become tense. A person may use the well-timed laugh to break that tense moment. At the same time, it is a very easy human expression to fake, and can be used to attempt to disguise stress from the casual observer. Nervous laughter can indicate that the topic under discussion is a hot or critical issue for the speaker, and it can be a sign of evasiveness or even deception.

Sighing

The verbal symptom of sighing has two general interpretations. First, constant sighing throughout a conversation indicates that the person is perhaps feeling a little sorry for himself in this situation, and may be feeling depressed. This is not to say that the person is suffering from clinical depression and needs counseling or treatment. It may be that his current frame of mind is one in which he would prefer to withdraw from the situation or just get it over with and move on to another topic. A single deep sigh from the person after there has been a period of strong resistance or generally aggressive behavior by that person suggests that the emotional or cognitive battle that he has been fighting within himself has ended. This person is ready to surrender to the other person's point of view. This is the sigh that criminal interviewers see frequently just before the person is ready to confess. This behavior is referred to as "acceptance." The person is no longer resisting the truth or the reality of his current situation.

Signs of Unclear Thinking

The presence of speech behaviors that indicate that the person has an "unclear line of thought" has been found to be a reliable signal that the speaker is being deceptive.[4] There are several examples of unclear thought that a subject can generate—omission of words, slurred or clipped words, incomplete sentences, repetition of thought, sentence editing, halting speech, and indirect ideas. Although these terms sound as if they are describing very complicated behaviors, they are in fact not all that hard to understand or identify.

When someone is talking and you notice that he seems to be leaving out a word here or there, you have just spotted an example of omission of words. It's almost as if the person would prefer not to speak the forbidden word or has some kind of second thoughts about the word he has chosen. Here is an example, "No, I did not after he left because I hadn't after we left."

Sentence editing has a similar appearance except instead of leaving out words, the person first chooses one word, then stops in mid-sentence and substitutes another word. For example, "I was yelling at her, well, not yelling but talking loudly." "I just touched her on the, well, just sort of brushed her on her shoulder." You also can see this happen when the person changes nouns, verbs, or pronouns in the middle of a statement. "We, we, I, I didn't do it." "We were taking, took her to her house." "He was asking, telling me to do it."

Slurring of words is a prime example of someone who has so many mental issues he is trying to address at the same time that he almost sounds as though he is suffering from a case of lockjaw. Slurring of words is a strong indicator that the individual is actively considering what the situation is, what his past statements have been, and how to proceed. When the speaker is responding to a direct question and is slurring his words, this is a strong indication of lying and you should take careful note.

The clipping of words is going to sound as though the person is speaking in a choppy or staccato form of speech. He appears to be putting emphasis on the first part of the word and trailing off on subsequent syllables. The person is more or less hesitating during the delivery of each word. This can also occur if the person is trying to sound convincing or add emphasis to the words to which he wants to call your attention. The person you are listening to is, in essence, performing or acting out his answer in order to emphasize something. Halting or uneven speech is almost a mirror image of clipping words. The person appears to be rushing some of the sentence and then slowing down on other parts of the sentence. This person is more comfortable with some parts of the sentence than he is with others. To the listener, it will sound as if the speaker feels a need to skip over or speed past a bad spot and move on to a point where he feels more comfortable with the story. This results in an uneven or broken sounding rhythm or flow of the remark.

Stress and anxiety can cause a variety problems in our ability to maintain clear thoughts and ideas. One of the problems we can experience is what we are going to call fixation of thought. Have you ever had a problem or task on your mind so much that you couldn't concentrate on anything else? You know, the kind of problem that keeps rolling around in your consciousness while you're sitting at the dinner table, and in the end you miss all the pleasant conversations? Perhaps you're sitting in front of the television watching your favorite show but your mind is off on a tangent thinking about this personal problem. When this is happening to a person, he may start repeating himself in his statements. You'll hear repetition of thought when the speaker starts repeating key words or phrases within the same sentence or oration. An example would be, "We, we never stopped there. I, I just, I just didn't want to stop, to stop there." Once again, don't forget that this is just a single cue and that it is not a definitive indication of deception. Be sure that you pay attention to other symptoms that may be exhibited in the quality of the voice as well as body language. The symptoms that are most significant are those that are timely in response to a question or similar stimulus.

The final examples of a person who is experiencing the problem of an unclear thought line is the occurrence of incomplete sentences and sentences that contain unrelated or indirect ideas. How many times have you asked someone a question only to have him respond in broken, incomplete sentences? That person is mentally sorting between several thoughts at once, trying to determine which one is the answer he wants to give. Now we all can get a little confused and distracted, but you'll want to watch for a situation in which a person's answer to a direct question is in incomplete sentences when the answer he should be giving is not complicated.

Don't forget that no one symptom of any kind is proof of truth or deception. You'll need to ask yourself, is this a change from what you have established as the person's normal pattern, and are there other symptoms that contribute to a cluster of behaviors?

A similar behavior can be seen when someone is responding to a question that you have posed to him and his answer seems to be totally unrelated to what you have asked. You may even notice that parts of his statement don't seem to be connected in thought or idea to each other. This person is really under some severe mental stress. He is having an extremely difficult time in deciding how to edit what he should or should not say in response to your inquiry. His emotions may be running very high about the issue, but he is trying to hide that from you and avoid leaking that information in his statements. The mental stage where the person is trying to prepare an answer is in total disarray and his attempt to sort out his thoughts and feelings are reflected in his answer.

Speech content accounts for only 7 percent of communication, but it is the most potent.

Speech Content

Of all the communication tools that I have, the content of my speech provides the smallest percentage of the total—about 7 percent. That 7 percent, however, can be the most potent part of any message that I choose to project to those who would listen. My nonverbal behavior, voice quality, and clarity may provide the visual and some of the auditory information about my ever-changing emotional status as I deal moment by moment with the daily issues of my life. If these things provide a glimpse of my internal emotional reactions, then the content of my speech represents the lines of code that represent the cognitive process of my thoughts. Within these lines of code may be buried the motives that result in my deceptive communication. By identifying and deciphering these lines of code, the listener can gain a glimpse into the ideas and thoughts that I am processing mentally. Particular patterns of speech content will occur in different situations. Shortly, we will be looking at the five reaction behaviors of bargaining, anger, depression, denial, and acceptance. Each of these can be recognized through a certain pattern. Suffice it to say, for now, that you will always be considering speech content—the words a person is speaking—as an important part of any conversation.

NONVERBAL
Communication

Y ou will remember that earlier we stated that a person who is speaking concentrates more on his verbal output than he does on his nonverbal behaviors. As a result, there are proportionally more non-verbal behaviors than there are verbal behaviors. It is estimated that as much as two-thirds of human communication is composed of nonverbal or body language behaviors. That's an awful lot of infor-

It is estimated that as much as two-thirds of human communication is composed of nonverbal or body language behaviors.

mation for the listener to watch while still listening. The good news is there is going to be a large quantity of information for the observer to work with. But the bad news is that a good deal of the body language that we are going to see is a symptom only of stress.

Few of those stress signals are going to be behaviors that can indicate whether the person who is speaking is telling the truth or is lying.

Digging through all the body language that a person can generate during a conversation in order to find the significant behaviors can be quite a challenge for any observer. Not only are body language cues that can indicate deception few in number, they are frequently surrounded by behaviors that are just the result of the person feeling stress, and, as a result, the observer can often be blinded by the stress signals. Picking out and sorting through all the nonverbal information is a lot like trying to carry on a conversation in a busy restaurant or bar while there is a loud band playing on stage. It's going to be hard to maintain your focus and concentration while keeping up with all that is being said in the conversation. The large volume of behaviors that are all being generated at the same time can increase the risk of misidentifying the meaning of some of the silent nonverbal actions. This is further complicated by the fact that most people do very poorly at accurately isolating and diagnosing nonverbal behaviors associated with deceit. Some of the behaviors that people traditionally rely upon to help them spot when another person is lying are frequently unreliable or inaccurate.

> **Look for body language symptoms that conflict with one another or a body language that disagrees with the speaker's verbal cues.**

Another drawback to the amount of body language you will have to observe during a conversation is the amount of work it takes to spot and isolate the symptoms. Needless to say, it can be very labor intensive. In one research project, it took trained observers an average of forty-five minutes to diagnose the body language of the subjects in two minutes of videotape. It took other observers only fifteen minutes to diagnose the verbal symptoms of the subject in the same two minutes of tape.[5] By the time we try to analyze all the nonverbal behavior, we may have missed the important content of the person's speech.

Let's go back for a moment and talk about the good news regarding body language. Although there can be a lot of body language generated by a person while he is communicating, he generally does very little to try to filter, edit, or control his body language cues. Because we pay little attention to our body language symptoms in comparison to the way we control our speech symptoms, the nonverbal signals often reveal much about the amount of stress we may be experiencing as well as our emotional response and the strength of that reaction.

The largest amount of information presented through body language is associated with the person's emotional response to the current situation or the topic that's under discussion. We as the listener or observer in a conversation should be concerned about the amount and type of stress that the person may be experiencing. In order for us to deal effectively with the other person, we must identify and correctly respond to that person's current emotional and cognitive stress response behaviors if we hope to have any productive communication with him.

If you know what to look for as an observer of body language, the information can be very valuable to you. One way to use body language to help you determine if someone is being deceptive is to look for contradictions. Note body language symptoms that disagree or conflict with other body language symptoms. The other method is to watch for body language that disagrees with the person's verbal cues. We refer to this type of disagreement between symptoms as a contradiction. Contradictions are typically very significant when trying to identify possible points of deception during personal communication.

One way to think about the significance of nonverbal behavior and how to read it accurately is to think of the various behavior signals as being like gauges on the dashboard of your car or truck. Your vehicle gauges provide information about how much gas you have in the tank, the speed at which you are traveling, oil pressure, water or engine temperature, the distance you have traveled, the revolutions per minute of the engine's cam shaft, the radio station to which you are listening, seat belt light, and so forth. In other words, the gauges tell you how the vehicle is performing by giving you a visual representation of the internal operations you are unable to see. Those same gauges let you know when the vehicle is operating outside what should be its normal range. For example, the engine light may come on when the engine has died even though your car may still be rolling forward.

Perhaps you look at your speedometer and see that you are going 35 miles per hour, you look down at the gear shift and confirm that you are in third gear, and a glance at the engine tachometer tells you the engine is turning at about 6,500 revolutions per minute. What!? Something is wrong. The engine shouldn't be running at that high rate of revolutions when the car is in third gear and traveling at 35 miles per hour. In fact, you should be picking up some other clear signals that the car is not performing correctly, such as loud sounds coming from your engine under the hood, along with a large cloud of smoke. That particular configuration of the readings of your car's gauges and equipment suggests that the car may have a serious mechanical problem. It's not the gauge or gauges that are causing the problem, but the reading on the gauges represents the internal operations of the engine that you can't see.

Of all the body language signals that we generate during communication, we are more aware of the signals that we exhibit in and around the head than we are of other parts of the body.

Nonverbal behavior or body language is much the same. It is not the body language that you are seeing that's important, but what the nonverbal behavior is telling about what is going on inside the person on an emotional, cognitive, or mental level is important. When those gauges disagree with each other or show specific signs that the person is functioning outside their "normal" operating range, then something important is going on and needs your attention.

To carry the analogy of vehicle gauges on the dashboard of a car one step further, think of being able to read nonverbal or body language behaviors by combining all the behaviors into four simple categories or gauges—head, eyes, arms, and legs. As we explore the significance of various nonverbal behaviors, we are going to use these four body parts to group the various behaviors into their respective categories.

Head

Of all the body language signals we generate during communication, we are more aware of the signals we exhibit in and around the head than we are of other parts of the body. Because of this awareness, we are capable to some degree of controlling and even masking or disguising some of those symptoms, and therefore some of those symptoms can be misleading to the person who is trying to diagnose our credibility. The overall quantity of behaviors that are generated from around the head are numerous and appear on a relatively small scale in terms of their size. In contrast, the symptoms for other parts of the body tend to be fewer in number but appear on a much larger scale and are therefore more readily observable.

Head Position

To begin our observations of the head, let's first discuss the general positions in which a person may hold his head and their various meanings. The first of these positions generally denotes a positive message to the observer. That position is one in which the head is held at a slight tilt to either the left or the right. This position will remind you a lot of the position in which your dog or cat holds its head when it is listening intently to a new or interesting sound. It has basically the same meaning for humans. It is a subtle cognitive message that the person is in fact listening to the current conversation that is a positive sign for the observer. A school teacher or college lecturer will see this type of head posture when the student is paying attention to the speaker. This person is absorbing or inputting the information that is currently being presented to them. There may be times when you see that the person who is listening has his hand placed lightly to one side of the face as part of this listening posture. One additional point about this position which includes the hand to the side of the face: the person in this listening format generally does not use the hand to support or to prop up his head. If the hand is propping up the head, that usually indicates the person may be experiencing some boredom with the current matter under discussion. That person may also be drifting in his own thoughts, which are different from the topic under discussion.

Another head position is one easiest to describe with an illustration: do you recall a time as a teenager that you came home late? You know, that Saturday night you came in thirty to forty-five minutes after curfew and Mom or Dad was sitting there in the living room in the dark waiting for you. As you were driving home or riding in the car with your friends or maybe the date who was taking you home, you had already started making up a story that was designed to explain why you were so late. It may have been the story about heavy traffic in town. Perhaps you used the excuse that you didn't know that the movie was going to be over so late. Of course, it could have been the worst of all the bad excuses—that flat tire story. Then there you were standing in front of your parents reciting the story just as you had rehearsed it in the car on the way home. Did you look at the expression on you parents' faces? Well, probably not, because you were sure that they might see the deception in your eyes or in your facial expression.

If you had taken the time to watch their expressions, you may have very quickly spotted a facial expression that indicated they did not believe your story. You may have noticed that they stood there with their hands on their hips, head tilted down with chin drawn back into the neck. I bet you remember now, don't you? It was part of that look that said, "I don't really believe a single word you're saying," or, "You don't really expect me to believe that, do you?" What you would have seen if you had paid attention was a sign of denial or rejection on the part of your parents indicating they did not believe what you were saying. If you are speaking to another person and you observe this head position, you want to consider the possibility that the listener does not really accept your current statements. If another person is talking to you while exhibiting this type of head position, he does not totally believe or lacks conviction in his own remarks, and therefore you should be cautious about accepting whatever information he is giving you without examining it.

Facial Expressions

As the observer, I can make several observations by watching the changes or lack of changes in a person's facial expressions. First, I should be able to get some idea of what the person's current emotional response happens to be—anger, depression, and so on. Second, I can determine the relative strength of the emotion the person is experiencing. Third, with careful observation, I can learn to identify expressions that a person is trying to project or perform for my benefit or that are designed to mislead me. Fourth, I may be able to identify any emotional responses that a person is trying to hide or conceal. Finally, I can learn to decipher when a person is trying to perform one emotional response, but is in fact experiencing a much different and stronger emotional reaction.

I can determine the strength of a person's reaction emotionally by looking at the features of the face. Everyone's face is covered with multiple lines and creases, and the depth, appearance, or disappearance of those lines and creases change depending on the contraction or relaxation of those muscles with each expression. Typically, if whatever emotion the person is feeling creates very deep creases or lines, or extreme contraction of the facial muscles, the strength of the emotional response corresponds with the intensity of the expression. On the other hand, if the person is trying to express a very strong emotional message but the facial expression does not demonstrate the corresponding intensity, then he is not really as emotionally aroused as he claims verbally. Remember, each of us has individual levels or reactions, and what is a normal baseline behavior for you may not be anywhere near the same for someone else. Compare a person's responses on both the verbal and nonverbal level against the constant you were able to identify for him.

Let's suppose that you and I are engaged in a conversation of some importance and in order for me to have or gain some advantage, I need you to believe that I feel very strongly about some point. In order to convince you that I have a strong conviction about the point I am making, I may engage in a performance of an emotion based on facial expression as well as other verbal and nonverbal cues. This is a tricky area for many people to decipher accurately. People who have very good social and communication skills can be very persuasive, causing the observer to overlook the subtle cues that suggest the person's reaction is not genuine. Cues that the facial expression is being performed or is merely a shallow projection of emotion will be the disagreement of expressions from various parts of the face. For example, there may be a huge smile on the person's face, but his eyes show little or no pleasure. Or perhaps you see a smile, but at the same time you notice that the person's jaw is flexing with anger. On a larger scale, the facial expression may not match the larger body language cues generated by the angle of the body, position of the head, or behaviors seen from the arms and the legs. I may be shaking your hand and smiling at you, but you notice a hard stare from my eyes, and the tone of my voice lacks any warmth. I'm not really that happy to see you or meet you, but in fact am more or less suffering through the inconvenience.

The reverse of performing an emotion or expression is to try to suppress or conceal an emotion or expression. You might refer to this as having a good poker face. Normally, as we are involved in conversation with other people, our facial expressions change throughout the conversation. They will change as we react to remarks made by the other speaker or speakers, and our expressions change as we express our ideas, thoughts, and emotions to others. For our face to be devoid of any of these changing expressions is as unusual as false or performed expressions. Should you notice that the person you are talking to is holding his poker face, he is doing his best not to reveal important or necessary information regarding his personal cognitive and emotional reaction to the topic at hand. He may perhaps not wish to disclose to you that what he is verbally expressing is not what he really thinks or believes, and he is therefore being less than honest with you.

Another way to decipher these concealed expressions is to remember that the more we try to repress a normal emotional response, the more likely it is that we will leak that information from some other source. Although I may be very stone-faced, you may see that my hands, arms, and legs are being very expressive in their movements. Perhaps you will notice a change in the quality of my voice while I am speaking and the words I choose reveal a strong emotional response. When we do not attempt to interfere with our normal, open flow of communication with others, all our verbal and nonverbal signals exhibit agreement and harmony. Any attempt we make to disguise, mask, or falsify those expressions disrupts the normal balanced harmony of our communication. Among these signs of disruption are the indicators that suggest stress or deception.

Hands to Head

Later in this chapter, we will explore the various actions of the hands and arms in greater depth. For the moment, however, I want to address the meaning of the hands as they touch various parts of the face and head. Contact made by the hands to four prime areas of the head also act as a form of concealment, not unlike what we discussed earlier. Pay attention to a person's remarks if you see that his hands are moving around his mouth, nose, eyes, or ears at the same time. These will appear to be in the form of either subtle or even outright covering of these areas. These types of hand actions are referred to as "negation behaviors" in that they neutralize or cancel the meaning of the expression. Studies of deception that include cataloging these cancellation behaviors by the hands indicate that they are frequently associated with moments of deception.[6] These cancellation behaviors range from the very crude to the very sophisticated and from the subtle to the very obvious. For example, blocking or covering the eyes could be as subtle as a gentle scratching of the corner of the eye or eyebrow or as obvious as totally hiding the eyes and even the face with one or both hands. Hand activity around the ears might include lightly touching or scratching the ears, playing with earrings, or all out digging down into the ears as if mining for gold.

Watch for the moments when a person engages in some hand to head contact that partially, if not completely, blocks or covers the eyes, ears, mouth, or nose. It appears that to some degree we may be subconsciously aware that we might accidentally disclose our deception from some outwardly observable action from these areas so we attempt to cloak their appearance by covering them or shielding them from the view of others watching and listening to us. This is not to imply, however, that every time a person touches his nose, for example, he is lying. One of the training videos I use in teaching detection of deception to law enforcement interviewers is the interview of a twenty-seven-year-old man. He and his brother were arrested and convicted for the burglaries of nearly two hundred drug stores in five states in an eighteen-month period. During his interview, the young man constantly put his hand to his mouth. For any other person, that might be a strong sign of deception, but for this young man it is his normal behavior. It is not until his hands move to cover his eyes, his ears, or to cover his whole face that his hand behavior becomes a sign that he is being deceptive. Don't forget to establish the baseline or constant pattern of behavior for each person and look for the changes in the pattern.

Of the four prime targets for the hands going to the head, the two favorites appear to be the mouth and the nose. There are numerous theories as to why these two locations are the most popular, the most prominent of which is the one I mentioned above in which the hands are used to mask or hide behaviors. In any case, for whatever reason, when the hands go to the head during deception, there is a good chance the eventual target will be the mouth or nose.

Blocking the mouth with the hands could loosely be interpreted as an attempt to control or block unwanted verbal output, however, the mouth can be blocked or obstructed with much more than the hands. One way to help avoid disclosing any significant information from the mouth is to put on a big smile. If you remember, we called this a "performance" symptom during which the speaker is trying to mislead the observer's impression of the significance of the comment. This is when you would notice that other points of expression from the face don't match or that speech and the other nonverbal cues fail to conform to the facial expression.

But there are other ways I can block or cover my mouth and the list is limited only by my imagination. For example, putting objects in or around my mouth can serve the same purpose. I can chew on pens, pencils, paper clips, fingernails, cigarettes, cigars, or pipe stems and accomplish the same thing. During investigative interviews, I have observed subjects also putting necklaces in their mouths as well as corners of file folders, purse straps, chewing on shirt or blouse collars, hair, mustaches, ear pieces of eye glasses or sunglasses, the string ties from hooded sweatshirts, and have even observed subjects who chewed on the collar of their undershirts. You also observe the person chewing on or biting his lip or even chewing on his tongue as a way to try to control his speech. As you can see the list can be endless but the result is the same.

The nose, apparently because of it's close proximity to the mouth, is also very stress sensitive when we are being deceptive and may serve as a substitute target for contact with or blocking the mouth. In fact, the nose may be chosen because the gestures are less obvious. Watch for the moments when your son finds his nose during a conversation. Now this does not include the child who is young and immature and starts digging in his nose at about the same time you expect him to display his best manners in front of your boss. These are more subtle actions such as gently touching or brushing the nose. In some cases, you may observe the hand-to-nose contact to be in the form of rubbing the nose, scratching the nose, or even pinching the nose closed. Take into account the possibility that this person suffers allergies or that the air may be very dry. Just remember that no one symptom by itself proves that the person is being deceptive.

Eyes

Eye Contact

One of the most enduring beliefs about human behavior and deception is that we can accurately diagnose the credibility of a person's statements by merely watching his eyes. In reality, numerous studies on deception have found that using the eyes to identify deception is very unreliable. Some of our misconceptions center around the amount of eye contact a person maintains with the listener when he is making a statement. This is based on the old saying that a truthful person can always look you in the eye. Numerous studies have shown that we do not maintain consistent eye contact during our conversations with others. If, for example, the topic under discussion is one with which we are uncomfortable, if we feel inferior to that person, or if we hold that person in contempt, we are likely to break eye contact during conversation. Behavior researchers studying eye con-

Using the eyes to identify deception is unreliable.

tact have learned also that the level of eye contact can vary based on cultural or ethnic background or can even depend on whether a person has an introverted or extroverted personality.

Neuro-Linguistic Programming

Another interesting belief about detecting deception by watching a person's eyes is a result of misinterpretation of the popular system of behavior therapy—Neuro-Linguistic Programming or NLP.[7] NLP was developed in the mid-1970s by John Grinder and Richard Bandler and has seen worldwide use by therapists and with reported remarkable results. One of the many facets of NLP is a therapy model referred to as "eye accessing cues." These cues are used to determine the preferred mental and communication representational systems for each person. The principle holds that some of us tend to be more sight-oriented in our thoughts and verbal expressions, while others are more auditory, or hearing-oriented, while yet another group is described as being kinesthetic, or feelings-oriented. One way these preferences can be determined, along with several other methods, is by watching the direction of a person's eye movement during communication interaction. Once diagnosed, the therapist or counselor interacts on the same representational system as the client, thereby creating much higher quality and far more productive communication. In fact, it is important to mention here that becoming proficient in NLP theories and methods takes a lot more work than simply reading a book or two or attending a seminar. Becoming certified to use, much less teach NLP techniques and theories, takes extensive study, training, and internship, and only then would a person be considered for qualification as a certified practitioner, trainer, or master trainer, by the NLP Society. Therefore, people who have read about NLP and think they can analyze a person's eye movements are not really able to do so with consistent accuracy.

We can learn valuable information about a person's mental and emotional states by observing the changes in the eyes.

There has been widespread misinterpretation of eye accessing cues and there are a substantial number of people who believe that you can accurately diagnose deception by watching eye movement.[8] Unfortunately, among the many people who believe in this concept are law enforcement interviewers and interrogators. They have gotten the idea that they can decipher whether a person is being truthful or deceptive solely on the basis of whether a person breaks eye contact to the right or to the left. Nothing could be further from the truth and a large body of research into this belief has proven it to be an unreliable means for spotting deception.[9] In fact, one prominent body language researcher regards attempts by law enforcement interviewers to spot deception using eye movement as being reprehensible.[10]

That said, however, all is not lost when considering what we can learn by watching the eye behaviors of those with whom we are communicating. We can learn valuable information about a person's mental and emotional states by observing the changes in the shape or configuration of the eye and its surrounding features, changes in the type of eye gaze, the blink rate of the eyes, and the presence or absence of tears. Timely breaks in eye contact that appear to be a change from the person's constant of behavior and appear as part of a cluster can be signs of stress and possible deception.

> **Timely breaks in eye contact that appear to be a change from the person's constant of behavior and appear as part of a cluster can be signs of stress and possible deception.**

You should make note of the fact that this rule coincides with our other rules regarding diagnosing behaviors. In particular, we are looking for changes from the person's normal or constant of behavior and most important those changes must be part of a cluster of symptoms. Changes in eye behavior alone are not reliable by themselves for diagnosing deception, but when combined with other cues of stress and deception, the changes can help us diagnose the underlying meanings of a person's behaviors.

Eye Appearance

While involved in a conversation with a friend or family member, pay attention to the appearance of the person's eyes. By appearance, I mean how the eye looks or the general shape or configuration of the eye and the features that surround the eyes. If you should notice that the eyebrows are raised extremely high along with the open appearance of the eye and its features, then your subject is experiencing shock or surprise. At the same time, some people will demonstrate an interesting eye behavior known as *san paku* (pronounced *sahn-pahku*) or showing three whites of the eyes. Take a look at the eyes of your spouse or friend. Notice that there are generally two white portions to each eye—one on the inside closest to the nose and one on the outer boundary of the eye. When some people are frightened, shocked, surprised, or experiencing extreme fear their eyes will show three whites and in some cases four. The third white of the eye is seen above or below the iris. When showing four whites, the white is visible both above and below the iris. At the same time, you are likely to notice that the eyebrows are raised very high above the eyes. This particular topic or situation is creating a great deal of stress for that person.

On the other hand, you may notice that the eyes and surrounding features take on a much softer look. In this case, the features of the eyes have a more open or rounded appearance. The muscles around the eyes are more relaxed, as well as the cheeks and most likely the rest of the features of the face. The eyebrows also may appear to be a little more elevated than normal. This expression is observed often when a person is experiencing some degree of emotional pain or depression. It also can be seen when a person is working through a bargaining response to the issue and is trying change the other person's perception of himself or what he has done or plans to do. It is meant to appear that the person is being very open and genuine, but in fact he is still being evasive to some degree.

Crying can occur with any emotion, especially if the emotion is particularly strong.

Tears and Crying

It would probably be appropriate at this point to talk about tears and crying. We generally think that when someone is crying, he is feeling pain and depression. That of course is quite true but it is not the only time you may observe tears and crying. Crying can occur during any one of the five stress response behaviors that we will be discussing—

anger, denial, bargaining, depression, or acceptance—and especially if that particular response being experienced by the person is very strong. Perhaps you know someone who cries when he is very angry. This is frequently seen when the anger is caused by some form of emotional hurt inflicted, or thought to be inflicted, by someone else. Listen to the content of the person's speech and you will hear the anger being expressed regarding the hurt.

Crying can occur also when a person is having a very difficult time with the current reality of events. His words and behaviors are those of denial, but the reality is intense and upsetting. This person may be expressing frustration or the feeling of being overwhelmed. We may see crying occur also when a person is trying to use tears as a means to gain our compassion or sympathy. Every parent can relate to this type of crying. A child looking for attention may whimper or cry.

Adults may use the same tools but in a far more sophisticated manner. For example, by conjuring up some tears or crying maybe I can get the cop to feel sorry for me and I won't get a traffic ticket. Maybe the professor will cut me some slack after I turn in my term paper late. Perhaps I can over-exaggerate my injury or pains just a little to get some sympathy from the good-looking ladies out on the ski slope. The results are the same—I have successfully changed the tone of the conversation and have gotten someone to feel differently about me. My success at getting sympathy or attention is going to depend on my performance, and I use all the resources I can think of to accomplish that goal, including tears.

Deliberate Eye Contact

We have explored already to some degree the idea that the amount of eye contact a person maintains when talking is not a consistently reliable means by which to determine truth or deception. This does not mean, however, that the person who is doing the speaking is aware of that fact—he may believe quite the opposite. Believe it or not, it is possible for eye contact to be too good. We usually see this type of behavior occur under two primary situations. First, the person who is maintaining strong or very stable eye contact may in fact be trying to maintain control or dominance over the person with whom he is talking. This is not quite the same type of control we exert over another person if we are using anger or aggression. The listener who is the target of this type of eye contact generally is going to have the feeling that he should not even think of challenging the accuracy of the other person's statements. It's almost as if the speaker is saying nonverbally that you should not even consider questioning him.

Many of the breaks in eye contact that occur are just signs of stress.

On the other hand, the second reason the speaker may maintain steady eye contact is because he thinks that, in order to be believed, he must look you directly in the eye. By looking you directly in the eye, he hopes to prove to you that he is being completely honest. This type of response can provide the skilled observer with a valuable clue. If we are following one of the basic rules regarding observing behaviors, we will notice that there has been a change in the person's constant. We should have established already some sense of what the person's normal or constant of behavior has been, and, therefore, when that person starts making what appears to be deliberate eye contact, we should classify the behavior as a significant change. In this case, as the person tries to perform a behavior which he hopes to have interpreted as a sign of being honest, he may in fact be providing a very clear signal that he is trying to cover something up. Behaviors of this type are called "performance cues." These are best described as an attempt on the part of the speaker to hide a true emotion by disguising it or covering it up with false behavior. Designed to give the outward impression that the person "acting" does genuinely feel strongly about what he is saying, these performance cues do just the opposite and are frequently associated with deception.

Blinking

Most of us do not consider blinking to be very significant—merely a biological function controlled by the autonomic nervous system. It is a necessary behavior for the proper function and care of our eyes and is really taken for granted. Depending on our physical environment, lighting, and other factors, we generally blink on the average about once every five or six seconds. Factors that account for variations in a person's blink rate would include wearing contact lenses, dryness of the air, allergies, medications, and a multitude of other variables. What is interesting, however, is that blinking has been found also to be tied to the amount of mental stress we are experiencing and our blink rate under stress conditions apparently coincides with how fast the brain is processing information. After establishing what may be a constant in the blink rate pattern for a person, pay attention to any changes that may occur. An increase in the blink rate suggests that the person is thinking rapidly. The person, for whatever reason, is quickly creating and evaluating his thoughts as he prepares his message, and this is a good sign that he may be undergoing a change in the level of mental stress he is experiencing.

Don't forget that not every break in a person's eye contact means that he is being deceptive. Many of the breaks in eye contact that occur are just signs of stress. This does not, however, rule out that there are some breaks in eye contact that are associated with clusters of behavior consistent with deception. We mentioned earlier that perhaps a person may try to disguise signs of stress or deception. One of the ways he may do so is by using his hands to cover partially or to block his eyes or other parts of the face. A buddy you work with might try to disguise his break in eye contact by turning his head away and appearing to be distracted by something in the distance while he's answering your question about sick leave or what the boss said about the upcoming vacation schedule. Perhaps the salesperson starts stalling, answers in incomplete sentences, and turns his face partially away from you or stares down at his desk when you ask if the service department handles all the warranty claims you might make on your new boat. These are all examples of clusters of behavior suggesting that there is a high probability the person is being deceptive. Don't forget to pay attention to the timing of the occurrence of these clusters. These behaviors don't just happen in a vacuum. They happen when the person is reacting to some specific question or remark you have made.

Arms

Crossing the arms has been one of those behaviors that everyone seems to believe suggests that a person is closed to communication or may in some cases be exhibiting a sign of deception. The crossing of one's arms can suggest sensitivity about an issue but then again sometimes crossing of the arms just means a person is crossing his arms. Once again, we have to learn to isolate the behaviors based on subtle combinations as well as timing. Remember that earlier we established that behaviors are going to be timely—they will be in response to some form of stimulus and we need to recognize what stimulus caused the change to occur.

Only a very small number of hand and arm behaviors are associated with deception.

When trying to diagnose the meaning behind why a person is crossing his arms, we need to pay attention also to other nonverbal messages and any verbal clues that may be occurring at the same time to accurately decipher that person's emotional and mental state.

In our discussion regarding the arms, we also are going to include the shoulders and the hands. The large majority of arm and hand behaviors you may observe in a person are going to be associated with adjusting to the changing levels of stress the person may be experiencing. Only a very small number of hand and arm behaviors are associated with deception. The deception behaviors are more likely to be associated with another verbal or nonverbal behavior or another part of the body as opposed to individual actions or movements. Once again, you as the observer of someone's nonverbal behaviors can be distracted easily by a lot of these arm and hand movements to the point of assuming that all such movements mean that the person is lying.

Shoulders

As a starting point for this part of our exploration of the body we are going to begin with the shoulders. There are not really many cues and signs from the shoulders, but they can contribute to our efforts at decoding someone's emotional and mental processes. First, as you interact with someone, notice the position of the shoulders while you are facing the person. Are his shoulders generally parallel to the position of your shoulders? If so, then there is a decent exchange of information and the other person is emotionally and mentally involved or participating fully in the conversation. If you see his shoulders rotated or turned away from you, the message is that he is not emotionally or intellectually involved or doesn't want to be involved in the conversation. Pay particular attention to the moment the rotation of the shoulders occurs. The turn or rotation usually occurs during the point in the conversation when your friend is rejecting your point of view. The conversation may be addressing an issue he doesn't want to deal with or is very sensitive about. If you see the rotation occur while he is talking, it is usually a form of rejection of his own statement and the person probably is not fully committed to his answer or doesn't really believe the answer himself. In this case, you also should not place full confidence in the statement—it may be at least partly if not wholly untrue. You will often hear of this type of posture described as "the cold shoulder."

While observing the movements of a person's shoulders, notice if the person appears to shrug his shoulders or if the shoulders appear to drop and even roll forward. Each of these shoulder positions has different meanings that are important for you as the observer. The shrugging of the shoulders generally means some form of rejection.

For example, should I shrug my shoulders while you are trying to make a point and you require at least some form of acknowledgement from me, it suggests that I don't really agree with you but may not be willing to openly express my disagreement. On the other hand, should I be responding to you after being asked a specific question and my response includes a shoulder shrug, I don't really believe my own remarks or I have little or no conviction in my answer. This can be a sign of evasion or even deception on my part.

How a person positions his shoulders during interaction with another person can tell you a great deal about his feelings regarding the person or the conversation. Once again, these are behaviors that can be very subtle and, for the most part, the person exhibiting these changes does so unconsciously. We are going to classify the shoulder movements into three general groups—swiveling the shoulders, raising or shrugging the shoulders, and dropping the shoulders.

When we are thoroughly engaged or interested in a conversation with someone, our body has a tendency to align itself parallel to the other person. If there are three or more people engaged in conversation, the position of our bodies and shoulders adapts accordingly. The position of each person's body contributes to what would appear to be a circle if you were to view the participants from an overhead position. However, if the conversation involves a topic that one person finds uncomfortable or if he strongly disagrees with a particular point of view, watch for that person's shoulders to turn or swivel away from the group or the other person. It would appear that he is almost pointing his shoulder at the person or group that is being rejected. You may notice this position change as the person continues his conversation. For example, as your boyfriend tries to make a point in his argument, you will see his body align in the parallel shoulder position, but when he is listening to a point of view with which he disagrees, you will see the counter shoulder position indicating rejection. If you are the person doing the talking and you observe this body position on the person you're talking to, you need to change your line of argument because the other person does not agree with you. This body and shoulder position can indicate also that the other person feels contempt toward you for some reason. You need to consider the past history of the relationship you have had with this person because some bad feelings of a past experience have risen to the surface. This might be a good time to clear the air.

The final shoulder behavior we are going to discuss is one that we will label as "body cascade." In this configuration, you will observe the person's shoulders drop and then hunch over or roll forward. The shoulders will remind you of water cascading over a waterfall or the crest of a wave as it starts to break on the shore. The mental and emotional state of the person you observe exhibiting this type of movement is strangely similar to these analogies. The definition of this particular position has two primary meanings, and, if you are not careful, you can make an incorrect assessment. Should you observe

How a person positions his shoulders during interaction with another person can tell you a great deal about his feelings regarding the person or the conversation.

this behavior in a friend of yours, you may be seeing a person who is moving into depression. On the other hand, it is seen also in a person who has moved toward acceptance after having been in a strong rejection frame of mind over an issue for some period of time or at least during the preceding discussion. The fact that this one behavior can be misinterpreted so easily highlights why people can be misled by the ability to read body language. It points out the folly of trying to read or diagnose the credibility of someone's remarks by observing or diagnosing only one area of his behavior. To be the most accurate in our task of diagnosing truth and deception, it is more prudent to look for redundancy or repeated behaviors from a person. That is why one of the most important rules regarding the accurate interpretation of verbal and nonverbal behavior is that we must make our diagnosis on the basis of clusters and not just on single symptoms.

In order to verify the accurate diagnosis of the shoulder collapse or body cascade as depression or acceptance we need to look for confirmation from other verbal and nonverbal cues. First of all, there will most likely be other nonverbal cues of either depression or acceptance. For example, you may see a sad facial expression, creases or worry lines in the forehead, downcast eyes, and so on. The person also may have had his eyes cast up toward the heavens in what is known as a "mercy stare," or you might see the hands to the face and rubbing the point of the chin, which also are signs of possible acceptance.

An extremely good source of this information is to listen to the person's verbal comments. If the person is experiencing depression, we are going to hear remarks from the person about how depressed he feels or that he feels bad. He may well mention all the problems he may be having on a personal, mental, or business level, or the problems he is having with his health. On the other hand, if a person is in acceptance, his remarks are going to be more conciliatory in nature. You will hear comments from the person that suggest he is looking for some way to resolve the rift that exists between the two of you. More specific details about these types of verbal cues are in the upcoming section on verbal behavior covering depression and acceptance. When trying to sort through deception or resistance from a friend or spouse, you need to be patient and non-threatening in your behavior if you hope to achieve any form of resolution in the conflict.

Hands

There are three main categories of general behaviors that the hands can exhibit and the number of variations in each category is almost endless. Those three categories include emblems, illustrators, or adapters. Each of these types of behaviors has special meanings and serves a particular purpose in our whole catalog of human behaviors. It would be impossible to describe all the possible movements or actions in which the hands can be involved. It is easy to understand the significance of each of these areas if we can decipher what purposes are served in the use of each of these types of movements.

Emblems

Emblems usually have fairly straightforward meanings or communicate generally easily recognizable messages. In addition, when a person exhibits emblems, he is doing so with deliberate intent, although emblems can and do occasionally occur on a subconscious level. Emblems include things like shaking the head up and down to indicate approval or holding both hands over the stomach and rubbing to indicate the person is full after a meal. Holding one hand up and palm out with the arm perpendicular to the body is generally interpreted as "Stop," while gesturing with the hands in toward the body would mean "Come here." The middle finger extended is a rather well-recognized message of contempt, while one finger placed to the lips indicates that there should be quiet or no talking.

Illustrators

Illustrators are also a form of open or easily read communication behavior. These hand and body movements supplement or complement verbal communications and tend to enhance the listener's understanding or appreciation for the message. One way to describe these types of actions is to think of the performing street mime. The mime, without using words, "illustrates" ideas through body language and silence. Watching these types of movements on a person is almost like watching someone play charades. We can understand readily that someone is gesturing "small" because of the position of the finger and thumb showing the listener a very small space between the two. We could understand a slammed door through a vigorous reenactment using hands and body. You can imagine similar mimed behaviors that visually enhance the verbal description someone is giving.

Some people are more prone to illustrators than others. There has been considerable research into why there may be such a disparity between those who use many illustrators versus those people who use very few. In any event, it has been found that when a person shows a change in his pattern of either using many illustrators and then dramatically suppressing such symptoms or vice versa, it is likely to be a sign of evasiveness or deception in his statements at the time the changes occur. When you notice this type of change in someone's gestures, you probably want to begin to ask more pointed questions and delve a little deeper for the information you are trying to uncover.

Adapters

The final category that is included in hand behaviors is the one we have identified as adapters. The movement or lack of movement and activities of the hands in this category primarily serve the purpose of relieving stress. It is for that very reason that diagnosing the significance of hand behaviors can create a lot of problems for you as the observer. The first problem is the mere fact that there are so many different combinations and variations of these behaviors that they can distract us from paying attention to the verbal message. Second, although there are many of these hands behaviors, only a few of them are reliable in helping us identify when a person is being deceptive. The good news, however, is that we do not edit or monitor our hand behaviors or other body language symptoms with the same diligence as we do our speech symptoms. As a result, watching the changes in these hand behaviors will give you a reliable sense of when a person may be under a great deal of stress or discomfort.

The list of possible stress behaviors in which the hands can be involved is almost endless. The specific actions that we each use under stress are a reflection of how we have learned to cope with stress over our entire lives. Some of the behaviors are the culmination of our years of learning and can be affected by our social environment and socialization. Yet other symptoms may be genetically rooted. The key rule, however, is that although we all work from the same endless list of behaviors, the adapters we each use come from our own personal list of habitual or favorite behaviors. We are once again confronted with the reality that each person's responses and behaviors are unique to that person and no one single behavior is universal in meaning for all people. Remember the oft-repeated basic principle that we must establish the baseline or constant of behavior for each person and then look for the changes in that pattern. Those changes represent a change in the mental and emotional status of the person and can be a sign of stress and possibly of deception.

One of the most common adapters is grooming behaviors. Let's assume you are talking to someone at a social function and this person is new to the group. When you engage this person in conversation you may notice that if he is a little nervous about the attention he is receiving, he may demonstrate an increase in grooming behaviors. This might include smoothing the front of his clothing, adjusting his tie or shirt cuffs, touching his hair or mustache, adjusting his jacket or sweater, brushing his clothes, adjusting his belt, picking imaginary lint or hair from his clothing, and so forth. Other signs of stress can be revealed by the hands while the person is holding an object of some type or is busy playing with his

It would be impossible to describe all the possible movements or actions in which the hands can be involved.

hands or fingers. The greater the level of stress experienced by this person, the more active the hands will become while playing with an object. You may see the person increase the rubbing, stroking, and fidgeting with his fingers. Now, this doesn't mean that everyone will do something like this in a similar situation. Other people may feel completely at ease in the presence of strange faces and do not engage in these kinds of stress-related behaviors. But that same person may show some of these symptoms of stress when sitting through a performance evaluation from a supervisor.

One final gesture or movement involving the arms and hands is what we are going to call a "dismissal gesture." This subtle gesture is one that suggests the person does not wish to talk about or deal with some issue or topic. Suppose you are talking to your current boyfriend and the topic of a past relationship happens to come up. As you discuss this other person in your companion's past, you inquire about whether he still has feelings for her. Should you see him making some form of sweeping gesture with his arm and hand away from his body, it is an indication that he doesn't want to discuss the issue. The gesture suggests a desire to get rid of the problem, throw it away, or not deal with it. At some point in the future, you may need to delve into this topic a little further and find out why he prefers not to discuss the topic with you. It may be because he is unsure about the impact the former relationship has on his relationship with you. It may be also that he is still experiencing some mixed feelings about the past relationship that still need to be resolved. There are any number of innocent explanations for it, but it is useful for you to know that the person you are talking to would prefer not to explore the issue at the current time.

What you do have to be alert for, however, is that in the midst of all these stress behaviors a person could generate behaviors that suggest that he is being deceptive with you. This is what makes it hard to determine the credibility of a person's remarks when there is so much other stress activity going on. You may find yourself distracted from the most important nonverbal and verbal signals while you are paying so much attention to his hands.

Legs

The behaviors you can observe from a person's legs and feet can give you some insight about that person's current emotional status. It is a good idea to watch the other person's legs at least peripherally if you are looking for signs of stress. When you compare various areas of the body with each other and their level of significance in diagnosing body language, the feet and legs contribute very little to our ability to learn if someone is being truthful with us. A person pays little if any attention to what he is doing with his feet or legs during a conversation. If he has any conscious awareness of his body language and makes any attempts to control those behaviors, it will be limited to the upper portions of the body. This general failure to monitor the lower extremities means that you as a student of body language are going to get some very clear messages regarding a person's emotional stress state because that person will do little to suppress or disguise these behaviors.

The simplest leg or foot actions to observe when you are talking to your friend is to watch for when they start moving. It's almost as if the legs and feet are pressure gauges. General movement of the feet or legs tells you the person is experiencing an increase in stress. Those movements include crossing or uncrossing the legs or maybe even changing the direction in which the legs are crossed. Another way to think about the significance of the movements of the legs is to consider them to be a demonstration of the person's desire to flee the current setting or situation in which he currently finds himself. After all, remember that all the body language changes we see are rooted in the instinctive response of fight or flight.

A similar diagnosis of the meaning of body language can be made if you see other types of motion from the legs and feet. Have you ever watched someone sitting in a chair and noticed that his knees are bouncing up and down, or perhaps wobbling back and forth? He is just trying to dissipate some of his stress. This person is not the least bit relaxed in his current setting. I can recall in junior high school and high school myself and fellow students sitting in the classroom taking an exam. Invariably you would see someone in the classroom with his legs pumping up and down like the pistons of a high performance racing engine. Boy, were we sweating out that exam in Ms. Pyle's chemistry class!

If you pay attention to a person's feet, you also can see some interesting changes in movement or behavior. If the person happens to have his legs crossed, you may see his feet start wiggling or pumping in the air. This is a clear sign of building stress or of impatience. On the other hand, you may not so much see something the feet are doing as you will hear them. When some people become very impatient or angry, you may hear them begin to tap or even stomp their feet! You need to pay attention to this signal and try to determine if there are other signs of anger in the body language or possibly some verbal cues. We are going to discuss the appropriate responses you should make when dealing with a person who is angry. Among other things, a person who is angry is not going to be doing a very good job of listening to you or anyone else. You are going to need to find ways to get that person out of this anger phase before you are going to have any productive communication with him.

Legs and feet are very good indicators of stress.

There also may be times when the person seems to more or less withdraw from his surroundings or to feel a little self-conscious. When this happens, you may discover that he has pulled his feet up underneath his chair or crossed his feet at the ankles and then pulled them up under the chair. This person may have a fragile sense of self-esteem or perhaps may feel a little inferior, at least in this particular setting. You will need to do your best to reassure this person.

At this point, you may be wondering why we are even discussing the feet and legs when they seem to have very little to do with identifying a person who is being deceptive. First of all, there are some people who believe that the types of behaviors I have just described are undeniable signs of deception, when in fact they are not.

The second reason we are spending time talking about the legs and feet is because they are very good indicators of stress. When a person is exhibiting any of the various forms of stress responses we have discussed, we can learn a great deal about that person's emotional, and in some cases, mental state. As the observer, you can track a person's internal reactions to each individual issue the two of you are discussing. If, for example, a person is exhibiting stress behaviors in the form of anger, I know that our conversation will not be very productive. To improve the quality of communication, I need to deal with the person's anger and frustration first. In addition to learning which emotional or mental response the person is experiencing, we can learn how intense that response happens to be by observing body language as well as listening to the content of a person's speech along with the quality of the voice. Later, we will discuss the appropriate responses for you as the observer in dealing with a person demonstrating each of the five stress response behaviors.

There are some additional behaviors a person may exhibit that can tell you about his present frame of mind. For example, have you ever noticed someone to whom you are talking suddenly stretching his legs way out in front of him? At the same time, he may lean his body way back in his chair. You'll probably notice that this lean is away from you. In the majority of the cases, this can be interpreted as an indication that the person has little interest in your point of view or generally shuns the topic. You may see this position along with the person also crossing his arms with one or both fists clenched under the arms. This combination indicates that the rejection is far more intense. If the person assumes this position at the same time that he is responding to your question, there is a good chance the person is not being totally open with you, is withholding key information, or perhaps is being deceptive.

A clear stress signal can be observed when someone has his legs crossed. As we noted above, pay attention to the moment the person crosses his legs to identify the moment of key stress. If he has been sitting for some time with his legs crossed, watch for the moment his feet begin to move. If the leg is crossed with the ankle resting on the knee, you may see the foot begin to wiggle up and down. The faster or more vigorous the wiggling, the greater the stress. If the person has the legs crossed with one knee over the other, watch for the person to begin to swing his leg. Once again, the faster and higher the swinging action you observe, the greater the stress being experienced by that person. If the person has been swinging the leg comfortably during the entire conversation, you are just seeing a person exhibiting his normal behavior of being in a relaxed state.

By now, you should have recognized that the feet, along with any movements of the legs, are signs of stress but alone do not indicate deception. But while you may be watching these changes, you could be distracted from seeing behaviors from other parts of the body that are a much more reliable sign of possible deception. Don't focus on just one area of the body, such as the legs, to make your determination of possible deception. Look at all the movements of the body. In some cases, what may be very important is the lack of movements from an area of the body that has been very active. Don't forget to listen to the person's speech at the same time for any contradictions between speech and body language. These contradictions can be a strong sign of possible deception.

Don't focus on just one area of the body, such as the legs, to make your determination of possible deception. Look at all the movements of the body.

Body Postures

We have spent a considerable amount of time talking about individual movements and lack of movements from various parts of the body. Let's now spend a little time talking about the significance of the overall posture of the body. By posture, I am referring to the angle of the body as it relates to you, the person carrying on the conversation.

Think of your spine or backbone as being like the axis of the earth, running north to south, and on which the earth rotates. If you remember your early science classes about the earth, you know that the earth rotates on that axis in a westerly to easterly direction, which accounts for the changes of day to night and vice versa. The tilt of the axis toward or away from the sun is what causes the seasons to change from spring to summer, summer to fall, fall to winter, and winter back to spring again. Using these two concepts of movement, let's briefly explore what it means when a person's body moves the same way.

The first general statement we can make is that the movement of a person's body away from you is not a good sign. For example, should the person's body be leaning back away from you, think of it as an expression of the person's desire to move away or get away from you or the issue under discussion. A variation of this position is if you see the person leaning noticeably to the left or the right. It is interesting how often you will notice this lean will be toward some form of exit or other escape route from the room. This can easily be interpreted as a flight behavior.

The most important point about these leaning behaviors is to notice when they happen. For example, you may be talking with your teenage son about the importance of avoiding the use of drugs. At some point in the conversation, you ask if he knows if any of his friends has ever used or currently possesses drugs, and at that point you see your son begin to lean toward the door while at the same time denying any such knowledge. There is a high probability that your son has just been deceitful. Maybe you've just asked a member of

The movement of a person's body away from you is not a good sign.

your staff if he has made some very inappropriate statements to a customer and you observe him starting to lean heavily toward a door or exit while denying any such comment—he may have been deceitful to you. Remember, you are very likely to pick up some form of verbal cue at the same time you notice the body lean. You now can be assured that the behavior was not a random occurrence but may be part of a significant cluster of behaviors.

Now that we have discussed the idea that the body moving away from you can be a sign of rejection of you or the topic, or can be a sign of deception, let's consider what the opposite movements mean. If the person moves or leans in toward you, that is not necessarily a sign he is accepting you or your communication. In fact, it may well be a sign that the person is trying to control you, dominate you, or even intimidate you. When this occurs, listen to the words the person is speaking. Also pay close attention to the tone and quality of that person's voice for sounds of aggression and dominance. In this case, you can correctly assume that the person is responding with anger or aggression. If you see the person sitting rigidly and bolt upright in the chair, the person may very well be trying to control all of his movements and body language. He is being less than open about his true feelings and emotions in the current situation. If he is trying to hide from you what he really feels or what he is really thinking, what else is he trying to hide from you?

If a person moves or leans in toward you, that is not necessarily a sign that he is accepting you or your communication. In fact, it may well be a sign that the person is trying to control, dominate, or even intimidate you.

There are some more of these subtle flight behaviors that can be exhibited by the rest of the body. Watch for the position of the person's hips to change. If you notice the person's hips shift or turn away from you and toward an exit, this person is demonstrating rejection or escape flight behavior. Once again, timing can be important. If the movement happens at the same time as a person is responding to some inquiry made by you, there is a good chance that person is being less than candid. An additional variation to this position occurs when you see the person's legs move and very obviously point in a direction away from you. This is a further indication of rejection and avoidance. You may see also the person's feet doing the same thing—pointing toward a potential exit or escape. A sheriff's deputy or a police officer transporting a prisoner would be alerted by this movement to the potential that the prisoner is considering trying to escape from custody.

Overview

We covered a great deal of information in this section regarding body language and when it can or cannot help us to determine if someone is trying to mislead us or make some form of misrepresentation. The most important thing we have learned overall about body movements and position changes is that they tell us that the person we are observing is experiencing some form of stress. The type of body position change, movement, or expression can tell us how the person is handling the stress and how strong that response might be. Buried within all these movements, position changes, and expressions are some signals that can help us isolate when a person is being deceptive. We just have to know which of these elements fit into which category or subcategory of behavior. All deception signals are a form of stress, but not all stress responses indicate that a person is lying to you.

We have reiterated several times the importance of looking at all the behaviors a person exhibits during conversation and of not being swayed by individual or isolated behaviors. I've mentioned several times that we need to have a good understanding of each person's baseline or constant of behavior and then look for changes in each person's individual pattern. Each of us over time has developed our own set of preferred reactions when we become stressed out. There may be some stress cues that you and I have in common while at the same time you might have some behaviors that I may never use. By the same token, we also have a fairly consistent

> **All deception signals are a form of stress but not all stress responses indicate that a person is lying to you.**

set of signals that we use and reuse unconsciously when we are being deceitful. The key to remember is that each of these catalogs is unique to each person. In some cases, a person may exhibit a specific behavior that is a constant for him but that same behavior in the rest of the general population has a strong connection with deceit.

RESPONSE BEHAVIOR

BEHAVIOR

E ach of us reacts to the events that occur in our world in two primary ways—emotionally and mentally (also referred to as cognitively). These two reaction levels have built-in overload systems that are designed to help us cope with the various events that occur around us and that can cause us to experience stress. These overload mechanisms help us recover some form of balance or order in our lives. The multiple ways we react with emotion and cognition or thinking can be described in very complex psychological terms and our methods of using these mechanisms would tell a trained counselor a lot about our current mental health. In a more general fashion, we can get a sense of how a person is dealing with some current stressful event by watching his verbal and nonverbal communication behaviors. The behaviors fall into five general categories—acceptance, bargaining, anger, depression, and denial.

Some years ago, a doctor who specialized in treating cancer made some interesting observations about how her patients and their families dealt with the inevitability of death. Dr. Elisabeth Kubler-Ross documented the multiple reactions of her patients and their families in her book.[11] Her work made a big difference for doctors, nurses, counselors, ministers, hospice staff, and others dealing with patients and their families who were facing the reality of death. Years later, the National Organization of Victims Assistance used Dr. Ross's same findings in their efforts in treating and counseling crime victims and their families. We can find that these same sets of reactions occur in all of us as we deal with the events that occur around us and create varying levels of stress in our lives. A highly stressful circumstance that a person may experience occurs when he is deceiving someone about his behavior or himself and there is a risk that his deceit may be uncovered. This circumstance creates the uncomfortable prospect of being held accountable for the original actions, the deceit itself, and for all of the resulting consequences.

Of the five general reaction behaviors that I may exhibit in a conversation, four of them create some form of resistance to whatever the reality may be. Those four are bargaining, anger, depression, and denial. I may exhibit them in any sequence and many times during a single encounter.

Each of the five response states—acceptance, bargaining, anger, depression, and denial—is evident in verbal and nonverbal behaviors. Whenever you watch and listen to other people when they are communicating, you observe their emotional and cognitive reactions to a specific issue. The more relaxed and comfortable the interaction between the people communicating, the less pronounced these behaviors would appear. Watch two people under stress or when the issue between them is extremely important or significant to one or both parties and watch the change in the intensity of their responses.

Acceptance is the response state you are seeking.

These behaviors will almost jump out at you as you watch and listen. Accurate diagnosis of these behaviors is also an excellent tool for determining the progress toward resolution between the other person and myself. I can use my reading of these behaviors to determine how I should be responding to the other person and overcome the barriers to open communication between us.

Acceptance

Acceptance is the response mechanism in which we ultimately take responsibility for our actions. When you listen to a person in acceptance there is no attempt to alter any information. He does not attempt to change your perception of him, nor does he try to persuade you to perceive his behaviors as anything different from what they really are. You as the person communicating with him are not attacked or blamed, nor does he attack or blame anything or anyone

You must allow that people are going to do some editing of their remarks as a means of preserving social order. At the same time, you should not take the naïve stance that everyone always wants to be truthful.

else for what has happened or where he went wrong. This is the response behavior that police interviewers and investigators look for in their interview rooms. This is when the subjects of investigative interviews or interrogations are most likely to give significant admissions or confessions. It is not necessarily a goal in our personal dealings with others to get a confession from them that they have been lying to us. It is enough to stop their attempts to deceive you because you have successfully unmasked their deception. The fact that the person is now dealing with you in an open and forthright manner is evidence enough that they are in acceptance. This does not mean that you have defeated or destroyed them in a contest of wills or that you are now in control of the destiny of another person. It merely means you have gotten past the stressful or even deceitful part of the conversation and are now dealing with each other on an open and honest level. Acceptance is the response state you are seeking. When you see that the person you're talking to is in a state of acceptance, you can proceed with open, honest communication. Now that you know the other person has relaxed in the conversation, you can relax, too, and let the communication flow. You will want to honor the other person's willingness to face reality, take responsibility, and act accordingly.

One of the perplexing elements about detecting deception by diagnosing human behavior is that conceivably there are times when a person may be untruthful and the observer will be unable to identify any signs of deception. With this in mind, it would be hard for us to assume that a person is telling us the truth because we don't see any signs of deception. So now we have the problem of deciding how to tell if someone is currently being truthful or is going to remain truthful.

It will be fairly easy for us to tell when a person has moved from being deceptive about an issue to being truthful and accepting reality. Remember that the reason we may be capable of identifying and classifying signs of deception is because of the internal emotional and mental conflicts that are generated when a person is trying to deceive someone else. The symptoms of deception can be enhanced easily if the target of the deception is challenging all the deceiver's best efforts in maintaining his deceit. The more the deceiving person respects the lie-decoding ability of the listener, the harder it is to suppress the cues.

The main element of acceptance is that the person who has been deceitful has now surrendered to the fact that the deception has not been successful. When this happens, the person who was lying has a change of objectives from trying to maintain the lie to repairing the damage to his public image and preserving and rebuilding his own ego and self-esteem.

You must allow that people are going to do at least a little editing of their remarks as a means of preserving social order. At the same time, you should not take the naïve stance that everyone always wants and desires to be truthful. The best advice I can give you is always to expect the unexpected and be prepared to communicate in a way that discourages deception, uncovers it when it does occur, and creates harmony and openness in your relationships. Should you see signs of possible deception begin to creep into a conversation or relationship, the time to address the issue is right away.

Left unchallenged, the other person may feel that such behaviors will be excused and before long the relationship will begin to deteriorate. This is particularly important with close relationships.

When dealing with deception in a person who is part of our intimate or personal circle, we will behave differently than with someone who is in a public or social situation. With a member of the intimate or personal group, a high level of trust exists, so you'll mostly be reacting to something that happened and that you are trying to find the truth about. This after-the-fact reaction occurs as well when dealing with a person in the public group, although for different reasons. Since you don't have direct access to that person, you'll be relying on what you see in the news. You'll certainly want to draw your own conclusions and you may want to write a letter or send an email expressing your views, but you won't be handling the situation up close and personally the way you would, for example, with a child or other family member.

When you have succeeded in breaking down the person's rejection of responsibility for his behavior, and you begin to see and hear signs of acceptance, it is time for you to assure the person that what you disliked was his behavior and that he as a person is important to you. This is the point when a child will learn that he can survive mistakes and rebound from a setback by first accepting responsibility, being accountable for decisions, and then correcting his behavior. As a parent, you have to take the opportunity to correct the child's behavior, make him aware of why the behavior was unacceptable, and then provide him with knowledge of the appropriate behavior alternatives. To punish a child without an explanation of why is of no value. With an adult member of your intimate circle, you'll want to communicate all of your feelings and clear the air, then ask the person for the appropriate promises for future behavior. The two of you can then proceed to rebuild trust in the relationship.

When dealing with people in our lives with whom we may only have temporary contact, the goal of gaining acceptance is much different. In these cases, you want to protect yourself and others close to you from becoming victims. Once an individual realizes that you are able to identify his deception and that you will not tolerate being subjected to deceit, the relationship is going to change. If that person does not believe he can accomplish his objectives without being deceptive, he will then find another target. Should he commit himself to being honest with you, the interaction between the two of you will be healthier and stronger.

Here is an example of that dynamic coming into play. Perhaps you have had a minor car accident that was not your fault. The other driver offers to make reparations on his own so that his insurance premiums won't go up. He offers to pay you an amount that turns out to be several hundred dollars less than the real cost of the repairs. You ask him how he arrived at this figure, and he tells you he has called a friend who owns a body shop where the repairs can be done for that amount of money. You drive to the body shop, to find its appearance disreputable and the owner discourteous. So you call the other driver and indicate that you are uncomfortable with what he is proposing. For a few minutes, he makes some futile attempts to convince you that the quote, the body shop, and the mechanic are all on the level. However, there was something about the shop owner's behavior that made you suspicious. Also, you've made a few phone calls yourself to get an estimate on the repairs. The other driver's suggested cost is absurdly low, even if the mechanic is doing a favor for his friend. You maintain your confrontational approach but you do not accuse him of lying. Instead, you continue to insist to the other driver that the proposed solution isn't going to work for you; he must come up with an alternative course of action. At that point, he confesses that his friend, the body shop owner, was planning to do only partial repairs and then charge you additional costs if you wanted the remainder of the repairs done. This person has been deceptive throughout the entire transaction and attempted to cheat you on your loss, but because you were diligent, you are not going to fall victim to his deceit. If he now offers to pay the full price to a body shop of your choice, you have the option of accepting his new offer and trusting that you'll be able to collect from him, or you may decide to go through the insurance company where you won't need to have such a concern.

Verbal Signals of Acceptance

There are three general types of verbal comments that a person makes that can indicate that he is moving emotionally and intellectually toward acceptance. These are a punishment statement, a third-person statement, and a debt-service statement. Each of these is a little bit different in nature and the titles are nothing more than a way to help remember the general characteristics.

A punishment statement is actually a question about what kind of punishment can be expected for inappropriate behavior.

A punishment statement is actually a question about what kind of punishment can be expected for inappropriate behavior. For example, let's say you are a teacher and you have discovered that a child in your class may have cheated on an exam. You point out to this student the evidence that indicates that he has copied from another student—the same wrong answers, some error in a math calculation, or maybe even a cheat sheet found on the floor beside the student's desk in his handwriting. After a few minutes of arguing, the results of your investigation point out to this student that he is caught. He poses a question like the following:

- "Am I going to get a failing grade on the test?"
- "Are you going to talk to my mom?"
- "Is the coach going to find out about this?"
- "Am I going to get expelled?"
- "Could I take a make up exam?"

What if you caught an employee at your office cheating on his overtime? You might hear something like this:

- "Am I going to be suspended?"
- "Could I lose my job?"
- "Is this going to affect my probation?"
- "Are you going to dock my pay?"
- "Is this going to look bad on my next evaluation?"

Notice how in each case the person is asking about punishment.

The next form of response is what we are going to call a third-person remark. In this case, a person all but admits to having been deceptive, but he acts as if it were done by an imaginary person. He may make remarks that sound like this:

- "I didn't do it, but I'm going to accept responsibility so we can put this all behind us."
- "I'll take the blame for this just so we can get on with our lives."
- "Would it make you feel better if I just told you I did it?"
- "Do you want me to lie and tell you I did it?"
- "You don't want me to admit to something I really didn't do, do you?"

The final category is the one I refer to as a debt-service statement. This statement almost sounds as if the person feels that he can do a good deed to erase the bad one. He is looking for an option to pay his debt and get it over with. These people are around you in all aspects of life—from the contractor who built your house to your six-year-old who broke the remote control for the television—and they may say things like this:

> In a third-person remark, a person all but admits to having been deceptive, but he acts as if it were done by an imaginary person.

- "We didn't cause that toxic spill, but we'll help pay for the clean up."
- "My son didn't vandalize those cars in the car lot but I'll help

pay for the damage."
- "I didn't break it. Will you let me try to glue it back together?"
- "I didn't lose it, but I'll go try and find another one for her."
- "I'll just drop my claim, and we can forget the whole thing."

Nonverbal Signs of Acceptance

You have to be very careful when making an assessment of nonverbal cues of acceptance. The majority of body language symptoms that tell you the person may be moving toward acceptance can have almost the same appearance as the body language symptoms of depression. In my work in researching and teaching interview and interrogation, I have observed that this can be a common misdiagnosis. The best way to be sure that the body language phenomenon you are observing is truly acceptance and not deception is to rely on a cluster of behaviors that includes the verbal signals that we have just talked about. It can be very easy to mistake depression for acceptance. Make sure you listen for the verbal signals to be sure your analysis is correct.

There is one change that can occur in a person's eye contact that can suggest that a significant mental and emotional change has taken place. Once again, we must remember to be sure we have established the constant or baseline of eye contact for a person in order to be able to accurately identify any significant change. Notice if a person appears at least momentarily to direct his eye contact up toward the heavens. In some cases, the person will hold this position for what may seem to be a long period of time. The change will include the whole head and face appearing to turn skyward. We are going to label this head, face, and eye gaze cluster as a mercy stare. This type of cluster is very significant if the people participating in the conversation have been at odds on some major issue.

It can be very easy to mistake depression for acceptance.

The individual who has been in a state of mental and emotional resistance to the issues is now beginning to surrender to the reality that he is in a weak position. We don't normally see this behavior occur during the discussion of something general or trivial in nature. The conversation between these two people has been on a very personal level. In criminal interrogations, I see this occur frequently right before the subject confesses. It appears that part of the reason that the head and eye turned skyward is also a physical attempt to keep tears from starting to flow. When I see a cluster like this during an investigative interview, it's time for me to stop talking and to start doing some listening. As one of the two parties who has been involved in what has probably been a very intense, in-depth conversation with this friend or family member, it's time for you to do the same. Give this person the opportunity to express his thoughts and you may find that the conflict that had been going on between you has changed course. Be patient with this person and give him time to work out his feelings and thoughts with you.

If you see the blink rate slow significantly, the person is now involved in an extensive internal dialogue or is currently lost in his thoughts. The chance that he is paying strict attention to whatever is being said to him is highly unlikely. The person has focused on one specific part of your comments and is mulling over that point, or he is completely distracted with his thoughts. On the other hand, you may see the person start to blink rather slowly, and if you pay close attention you will notice that the blinking will appear to match the pace of your voice. For example, when you pause in your speech, you may see him blink. When you finish a sentence or comment, you may see him blink. He is now tuned into you and paying close attention to your comments. It's almost as if his mental computer has now synchronized itself with yours; his computer is absorbing the bits and pieces of data, and he is carefully evaluating the data. Congratulations! Your friend, co-worker, son, or daughter is now paying attention to what you're saying. The person doing this is in a form of acceptance, which is a positive response, and he is likely to be agreeing with you, or at least agreeing with most of what you're saying.

Dropping the shoulders and rolling the shoulders forward conveys a primary meaning and is exhibited in periods of significant depression, denial, anger, or bargaining. Importantly, the rolling shoulders may be taken as a sign that the stage of acceptance has been reached. For example, you and I may have been engaged in a very intense conversation with each of us expressing strong points of view. We have both been defending our position on the issue with great exuberance, each believing the other is wrong or even withholding information. Should you notice that I exhibit the shoulders collapsing and rolling forward, you can conclude that I may have reached the point where I am ready to surrender to your point of view. In criminal interrogations, this type of posture suggests that the person may very well be on the verge of confessing or at least cooperating with the interviewer. Once again, remember that no single action by itself proves anything. Look for other verbal and nonverbal signals that can confirm your diagnosis. Also remember that one signal does not mean the same thing for every person, nor will it be used by every person. You are going to have to establish the baseline or constant for each individual and look for changes from that constant of behavior.

Here is an example showing how a combination of verbal and nonverbal signals can indicate acceptance. I believe that the car salesperson has not been truthful about the history of the used car he sold to me. After I had the car for a couple of weeks, I noticed that when it rains, the windshield leaks. Attempts to repair the leak haven't worked. I finally learn that the car had been damaged in shipment and poorly repaired. I confront the salesperson with my complaint. Throughout our conversation, the salesperson denies ever knowing that anything was wrong with the car; however, he had told me previously that he personally inspects every car and even had said, "I won't put you in any car that I wouldn't sell to my own mother. I would never deliberately sell a damaged car." When it appears as though our long discussion will end in stalemate, I provide him with an out by suggesting that the windshield leak could have been an oversight and that a good businessperson like him

Be careful not to increase the person's stress level.

would certainly take care of any such problems if he could. He leans forward in the chair, opens his arms, extends them forward with his palms turned upward, and says, "I'm sure we didn't see any damage on that car, but we might be willing to take care of it for you. You're going to get the windshield fully repaired." Notice that the third-person statement is paired with a dropping of the shoulders.

The next four response states are the states you may have to move through before you get to acceptance. Keep in mind that when you are observing these response states, you are not necessarily staring in the face of deception. You are merely uncovering the fact that there is stress for the other person in either the topic you are discussing or in the way the conversation is going. You will want to be very careful not to exacerbate the stress and to handle the conversation in a way that will get the other person to acceptance and the two of you to an open and honest place from which to communicate.

Bargaining

Bargaining behavior is an attempt to disguise reality and is more or less a soft form of deception. We have taken a look at the reflection of the image of our actions or ourselves and have found that reflection to be unpleasant or one that, if seen by others, would be a hindrance in the furthering of our personal goals and objectives. After viewing this image, we may decide it is time for a makeover, and so we attempt to disguise the image and behaviors and put ourselves or our behavior in a better light. We attempt to find ways to have the other person draw personal parallels between himself and us. This helps the person identify with us on a very intimate and personal level and thereby find it hard to condemn our actions or us. Consider the following example of bargaining.

I am very interested in a job with a company that has recently relocated to my town. I know I don't have the necessary training and experience or college degree that the company requires for candidates, but I set to work on the application anyway. In the section requesting my place of residence for the last ten years, I write the address of my parents' home. The next section inquires about my educational background, and I report that I attended business school and have taken additional courses at a nearby university. In the space for work experience, I write that I worked for five years in the business office of a Fortune 500 company, then was self-employed for seven years doing business consulting for the U.S. government, with contracts in Kentucky and Florida. To bring my work experience record up-to-date, I write that I am currently doing contract work for the state that will be completed in approximately four months. Under personal goals, I indicate that I am anxious to get back into the corporate structure, where I can make full use of the skills that I have developed while operating my own business for the last seven years. Now, that sounds like a pretty good job application. I come across as a well-educated man who is an independent self-starter with a good deal of practical experience.

Bargaining is a soft form of deception, but no less harmful.

When you decode my well-written application, it reads a lot differently. I use my parents' address as my place of residency but didn't really live there, although I did have all my mail sent to their house. Yes, I did attend business school: I attended a couple of seminars, but I was never enrolled as a student nor did I graduate. I enrolled for one semester at the local university but dropped out after the first semester because of failing grades. I did work for a Fortune 500 company, from which I embezzled about $35,000 while working in the purchasing department. When I wrote that I left the company to become self-employed for seven years working on U.S. government contracts, I was really at the Federal Correctional Centers in Kentucky and Florida, serving out my sentence for embezzlement and mail fraud. I'm finishing the final portion of my current state contract, which is the five hundred hours of community service I received as a condition of my parole. Boy! Can I dress up a job application or what? I can make myself and my activities sound pretty good. This is a classic example of creatively disguising reality, or bargaining.

There are several keys to dealing with bargaining behavior. The first is to remember that bargaining can be characterized more accurately as evasion, which, as the above example shows, can be just as deceptive as outright lying. Second, bargaining does in fact have some elements of truth buried inside, although they are dressed up and disguised to look like or sound like something else that's not quite so offensive. The correct response of the listener is then to hear out the person's bargaining remarks. Give him all the time he wants and allow him to weave this disguise, all the while knowing that at the heart of the story is some truth. Temporarily listen to and agree with his re-characterization of himself and what he has done. In fact, you can help him carry the charade further by going along, using his terms and personal characterizations. Once the person has generally completed this charade and feels that he has succeeded in selling you on his version, take him back to reality by asking pointed, detail-oriented questions that fill in any gaps you have noticed in his story. Point out any contradictions, ask about missing information, ask that vague language be clarified in more specific terms, and you will successfully disable the bargaining technique.

Sometimes the other person may be using bargaining as a method of softening you up so that he can take advantage of the developing relationship at a later time. Later, should you suspect deception, you will hesitate to act or to trust your instincts, because you will feel that to do so, in some way, is to betray a friend. You can find this method being used quite often during the soft-sell sales technique. The salesperson finds out your personal goals and goes to great lengths to learn about and discuss them in detail with you. Those goals then turn into the very reasons that you should buy a particular product from him. If you decline, he will try to make you feel guilty. You had indicated that you really needed and wanted his product. Did you mislead that poor salesperson after he has spent so much time with you, gotten to know you so well, and done so much to help you get what you wanted? And now you don't want it? In the end, if his tactics have been effective, you will feel obligated to the salesperson, because not to buy the product now tends to make you feel like the bad guy.

What really happened in the situation? The salesperson misrepresented his emotional involvement in the relationship. He embellished his account of how much time and energy he has spent with you, learning about you as well as informing you about his product. Finally, he even has exaggerated your wants and needs. In short, he has been bargaining with the truth in order to deceive you and fulfill a selfish goal of his own, in this case, earn a commission. Whenever you hear a statement that sounds slightly exaggerated, embellished, or just not quite how you recalled an occurrence, be careful: the other person could be engaging in some form of deceit, which he hopes to pull off through bargaining.

Verbal Signals of Bargaining

Remember that bargaining is an attempt to disguise reality. The subject accomplishes this by trying to change the world's perception of the actions that he has committed and/or the role that he played in the event. In the examples described below, you should notice that the person is not directly denying what he has done or his role, leaving an element of truth in his statements.

One way we may try to deal with the reality of any of our inappropriate behaviors is to describe them in much more favorable terms or by using "soft words." For example, "stealing" may be referred to as "borrowing." A politician or other public figure may have lied but will say he "misspoke," or was "quoted out of context," "misinformed" or "mislead" the American public, or perhaps "shaded the truth." When the traffic cop stops us on the interstate when we are going 80 miles per hour, we're not "speeding," we're "keeping up with the traffic," "passing another car," "running late," "have to go to the bathroom," "the accelerator is stuck," or "the cruise control doesn't work." Our kids don't "hit" each other but perhaps will admit, "I pushed him." The kids who trashed the house were "just messing around." How about, "I wasn't yelling, I just raised my voice." A public figure may describe a sexual affair as one in which he was not "romantically involved." Notice in these examples that the person hasn't really denied what he has done, only altered the description of the actions using less offensive words or phrases that could cause the listener to misunderstand the true action.

A response may also be vague with regard to numbers, amounts, times, or similar measures. The person hopes that you will assume something other than the true reality. Below are some examples of minimizing:

- "There were only a few of them."
- "We didn't get many."
- "It was only a little while."
- "It's not very far."
- "There was just a little bit."
- "I didn't hit him too hard."
- "Just a little noise."
- "We weren't going very fast."
- "It wasn't too much."

In the bargaining examples above, the person has been attempting to soften or diminish the harsh appearance of his personal actions. In the examples that follow, the person will be trying to change the way that others perceive him, in the hopes of creating a more favorable impression or image. He believes that if you buy into his version of his identity, you are less likely to see him as a bad person or someone with bad intentions.

Soliciting Sympathy

A person may try to solicit your sympathy when he is in a tight spot in a conversation. Instead of a person who acted inappropriately or with malice, he wishes to be seen as some form of victim. For example, the boyfriend may admit he was "a little too friendly" (notice the softer description of "flirting") with that woman at the party because he had had a few drinks too many. The office manager who was arrested for embezzlement may blame it on his "problem with drugs." A man who is accused of sexually harassing female members of his staff may say it happened because he was "raised in an abusive home." For whatever I have done, there is some circumstance, illness, or societal or social pressure that has forced me to act out in some inappropriate way. If I can get you to believe that, then I'm not totally responsible for what I did.

Religious Statements

Another way I can remake the image you have of me is to have you see me as a person who answers to a higher moral authority. Because I hold myself to such a high religious standard, I am precluded from any of the normal human weaknesses. Now, generally these are not the types of remarks you hear from people who are truly faithful to their religious beliefs. A person of real faith lives a life of integrity and honesty that is obvious to all those around him and generally has no reason to remind everyone. Their lives are shining examples of character and moral integrity. I doubt any of us has every heard the Reverend Billy Graham say to anyone, "As God as my witness." I don't believe anyone has heard the Pope ever say, "I swear on the Bible." Following is a list of examples of religious remarks. This is just a short list of examples and does not include all the possible combinations that a creative person could invent.

Swearing oaths:
- "As God as my witness."
- "I swear on the Bible."
- "May God strike me dead."
- "My right hand to God."
- "Honest to God."
- "I swear on my father's grave."
- "I swear to God."

Religious behaviors or items:
- Displays or refers to the Bible while avoiding the issue.
- Quotes religious scriptures.
- Points out his religious talismans (crucifix, rosary, Sunday School pins, etc.).
- Shows photos of religious leaders, philosophers, or family.
- Mentions position in the church or with religious group.
- Asks to pray with or for you.
- Talks about religious convictions.
- Asks you about your religious convictions or beliefs.

Once again, remember that we are not talking about actions of dedicated people of true faith and religious convictions. True people of faith do not put on airs as a way to avoid having you see their true character. The kinds of religious behaviors or remarks that we are talking about here will be exhibited as a substitute for responding directly to the issue at hand.

Personal Morals/Upbringing

Remarks about personal morals or upbringing are similar to the religious remarks we have just described, but this time religion is not the key element. The primary element in these comments is associated with some other code of conduct to which I want you to believe that I adhere. I want you to assume that because I am of a special class of people, am associated with a particular group or association, have accomplished some goal, or am a publicly popular person, you should not question my statements. Similar to what we said about religious remarks that people use, people of good moral character don't have to tell you about their character—they live it all the time. Following are examples of comments meant to draw attention to personal moral codes or upbringing:

- "I was raised better than that."
- "I'm not that kind of person."
- "I am a veteran."
- "A former scout wouldn't do that."
- "I'm a good employee."
- "I'm a faithful wife/husband."
- "I belong to the (group)."
- "My daddy taught me better."
- "I'd never stoop to such a thing."

Bargaining can be done very effectively through verbal behavior, especially if the person is exceptionally persuasive. Teenagers can convince one another that what they are doing is not really wrong because no one is going to get hurt. I can make my girlfriend feel guilty about asking me where I was on that Wednesday night when I had promised I would call her but didn't. Your daughter's current boyfriend may act like a gentleman when you and your spouse are around and might even attend church with you on Sunday, but you'll have cause for concern if he is mistreating your daughter.

Here are two examples of how bargaining behavior works. The contractor whom you hired to build the new deck had seemed like a nice guy. Telling you that the work could be finished in two weeks, he put you at the top of the list. He even knows some of the people you know down at the American Legion. He casually mentioned being a veteran and having served in Desert Storm. However, your perception of him changes once you see the shoddy work he does and learn of the complaints filed against him at the Better Business Bureau.

Your company is considering buying a new piece of equipment for security purposes in the computer center. One possible option, a particularly high-tech product, is pitched by its inventor. He informs you that his device has been tested and proven able to preclude more than 95 percent of computer hackers. The inventor provides his credentials: he has a Ph.D. and was a police officer previously. He tells you not to give credence to the competitors who say his product doesn't work because they don't have the most modern equipment—they are just jealous. Later you may learn he was forced out of the police

Watch for plays to gain your sympathy.

department, has been convicted in state and federal courts for fraud, or his Ph.D. comes from a store-front college that sells worthless degrees and has nothing to do with electrical engineering or computer science. Maybe you should reconsider all of the claims he has made about his product. You also now understand why he was hesitant to put you in touch with previous clients or let you contact any of his business competitors.

Nonverbal Signals of Bargaining

People who engage in bargaining to accomplish their deception are most effective when they combine nonverbal cues with the soft words and various types of bargaining phrases described earlier. When used together, these two elements comprise a nice little bargaining package: the look to go along with the words, each component heightening the potency of the other.

For example, your children may be seeking your sympathy and will put on a pitiful look, hoping to melt your heart. The guy at work who wants you to work his shift so he can go to the track will buddy up to you and start acting like a real pal. He slaps you on the back, buys you a beer, or picks up the lunch tab, and he promises he'll return the favor by covering when you want to take off early for a long, weekend fishing trip. His promises might be as reliable as he is. Be careful and analyze his behavior for what it is, or else you are going to be burned just as a few other guys already have.

Excessive Courtesy

A person who is hoping to have you overlook his behaviors may act very, very courteously toward you after he has deceived you or intends to deceive you. The old saying, "You can catch more flies with honey than with vinegar," also applies to that person who hopes the world will overlook how he has mislead or continues to mislead those around him. Once again, this is not to say that common courtesy or socially appropriate behavior is a disguise, but you will want to be on the alert for unctuous or phony politeness, particularly if it is used to draw your attention away from the issue at hand.

There are people who will hide under the guise of being warm and friendly to help them escape responsibility for their actions. How could you ever believe this person would mislead you or lie to you? "You know, I'm not sure whether I believe him or not, but he's such a nice guy!" Just think of the smiling rogue and you'll have the right mental image of the game this person is playing. One excellent example of this kind of behavior is Eddie Haskell of the popular 1960s television show *Leave It to Beaver*. Eddie had a way of getting under your skin because he could really put on the air of the good kid when he needed to, but you knew he was doing it to cover up his real intentions.

Watch kids around Christmas or as their birthday draws near. It's amazing how good they can be or how their chores are always done so they can eradicate the memory of their less-than-stellar behaviors during the rest of the year. Examples of people playing this game are those who go way beyond being nice to you. They might give what is, in reality, very insincere praise. Sometimes these remarks are made in the hope that you might feel obligated to this person in the future and excuse his performance should it fall below expectations. You may feel that the person is constantly buttering you up.

For another example, have you ever been helped by a salesperson who is remarkably "touchy"—that is, she consistently touches your arm or hand when she wants to show you something—and friendly? She has a smile that appears too big and fake. Trying to come across as attentive to you and your needs, she tilts her head to the side at a funny angle when listening to you. She keeps nodding her head as if she's really concerned and exaggerates all her facial expressions. You are watching one of the best bargaining shows on earth! The salesperson who can get the customer to warm up to her can sell him anything!

Denial

Denial is a rejection of reality. As much as 90 percent of deception occurs in this response state. In order for this response to be effective, the person has to convince himself as well as those around him that what everyone thinks is the truth or reality is in fact a mistake in perception. What everyone thinks is the truth is not correct, and he will tell everyone what the reality of the situation really is. The thought process is, **Denial is the outright rejection of reality.** "As long as you listen to me and believe what I am telling you, everything will be just fine." If denial is going to work, it is all up to the deceiver. He must try to convince himself and everyone else to ignore the truth or to accept his explanation of the facts. The result is a great deal of work for the deceiver because his denial is going to need constant nurturing and attention.

Denial creates a paradox of thought. In order for denial to work, the person literally points out what everyone thinks may be the truth, then tries to convince them that they are mistaken. That he must point out the evidence to others in order to deny it is actually calling more attention to the very facts he is asking them not to believe.

For example, the sun does not shine in the daytime. It does not create bright light by which we can see everything around us clearly, nor does it warm us, the ground, and the plants in the garden, nor the air or the atmosphere. It does not cause the plants to grow, the flowers to bloom, my skin to become tanned, mud puddles to dry up, nor the clothes out on the clothesline to dry. If you think that's what is happening, you are mistaken; if you listen to me, I will tell you what is really happening during the daytime because it is not the sun you think is there.

This illustration is a rather simple example of denial, but that is the same mechanism used to deny reality. Notice that as I try to explain away everyone's perception that there is a sun, I was calling attention to the very evidence that indicates that it could be there.

For denial to work, everyone has to listen to and believe my version of reality, including myself. If you show any doubt in my explanation, I just work a little harder at trying to convince you of my version of the truth. The moment I see that I have started to win you over to my way of thinking, I have gained confirmation of my deception and you have just bought my lie. You have now given me the confidence that I need to believe that I can escape the consequences of my behavior. Each little victory just helps to strengthen my denial. If someone successfully attacks a portion of the complex denial system I have created, I merely work harder in that weakened area to protect myself from having to accept responsibility for my behavior. Once again, you see I must have an understanding of what the truth really is in order to continue to sustain successful denial. A person in denial needs to begin to believe the deception himself, so that he can be strong and persuasive in keeping up the building and repair process of denial. However, little glimpses of the truth generally shine through, giving the deceiver moments of insecurity, even if he was beginning to feel safe in the deception. Denial is a very fragile foundation, and requires a lot of work on the part of the deceiver to keep it shored up.

Denial really is at the heart of deception. It is in this frame of mind that a person creates, nurtures, and propagates deceit. Denial is the all-out rejection of reality. This is where you, as the target of the lie, have your work cut out for you. If you intend to overcome deception, you are going to have to venture into the jaws of lying.

We have discussed the characteristics of denial and how the mechanism of deceit involves the deception of self and others. It also was described as a paradox of thought in that in order for denial to work, I have to call attention to the very evidence that proves reality exists, and then convince myself and everyone else that it is not really there, it doesn't really exist, or that it doesn't really mean what they think it means. As the person who is the target of deception, the only way I can overcome this rejection of reality is to attack with reality. I am going to call attention to all the individual pieces of evidence that this person says do not exist to remind him that I can still see the reality. This type of attack effectively disrupts the liar's efforts to create a falsehood.

In order to overcome denial in another person, I must develop a form of attack that will be the most productive. My attack on denial is going to be custom designed to fit the general personality of the person who has decided to lie to me. If I determine that the person who is attempting to mislead me has an emotion-dominated personality, my attack will be one that has lots of emotional content to it. By emotion-dominated personality, I mean a person whom you could characterize as someone who is very sensitive to others or wears his heart on his sleeve. I'm going to be sure to point out the very personal aspects of the evidence of reality. I work slowly as I debate the facts of reality with this person and I avoid all hints or appearance of being aggressive. I'm going to be very patient and present my argument for the truth in a very orderly fashion while being sure to present the evidence in only very small doses. This person can become overwhelmed very quickly. I want this person to feel as if he is obligated to eventually tell me the truth. In other words, make it a guilt trip.

Should I determine that the deceiver is a sensory-dominated person, my approach is going to be not to pull any punches and to get to the issue quickly. This person is usually a very outgoing and strong personality and tends to be very persuasive, and he respects people who deal with him in the same manner. My approach is going to be direct, unvarnished, and specific. Be very businesslike and don't let things get personal. Don't bring up any point in your argument that you cannot prove or are not ready to defend. This person is going to enjoy the energy and challenge involved in the debate over the true nature of reality. Don't back off your point of view, but don't try to intimidate him or bluff him either because it won't work.

If I determine that this person is a logical-dominated person, I am going to argue the facts one by one. You are going to feel as if you are in a championship chess match. Every move is calculated and thought out first before acting. You must prove to this person that logic dictates what is true and what is fiction and he will only agree with you when your argument is sound. Don't be surprised if you get very little body language from this person because he doesn't get as upset or stressed out over the confrontation between your differing views of the truth.

Finally, if I determine that this person is an ego-dominated person, I will approach him with the facts only after he has tried to say the facts don't exist. This person does not like to get bogged down in details. He also has a hard time when he is confronted with the reality of his actions and accepting the fact that they may be wrong. He strives very hard to preserve the image he has created for himself. He would prefer to find fault elsewhere and then dismiss the problem as a tempest in a teakettle. The best you can hope for in dealing with deception in this person is not to let him get the best of you and fall under his spell, because this type of person is a very charismatic, dynamic personality. People frequently get caught up in their outgoing personality and the strong influence they can develop over others and wind up completely ignoring their flaws and mistakes.

The key to dealing with denial is to attack with reality. You are not going to stop people from attempting to lie to you, but you can take the opportunity of them succeeding at the game away from them. One of two things is going to happen when you are successful at continually disabling another person's attempts to mislead or deceive you. First, if this person learns that he cannot manipulate you or control you with his deception, he usually will go find someone else to victimize. It this case, you will be much better off without him. Or second, this person will learn that it is far better to deal with you honestly and will continue to do so as long as you deal honestly with him. This is your ultimate goal: to develop, build, and nurture a friendship or relationship that is built on mutual respect, trust, and honesty.

Verbal Signals of Denial

In my earlier discussion of denial, I mentioned the fact that this is where the cognitive attempts at misleading others is in full swing. These verbal symptoms highlight the fact that the person is actively creating lines of thought that are designed to deceive both himself and you as the listener.

Memory Lapses

Everyone forgets something now and then, but we rarely forget an event that could be classified as significant. Not many of us will remember what we had for lunch a week ago today. Now that's assuming, of course, that we don't eat the same thing every day. But, would we forget what we had eaten for lunch on the same day last week if that was when we had lunch with a movie or television star? Well, that may depend on who is asking about it, and hence begins the denial! So you must first classify the event or information we are asking about. Is it something that a person would under most circumstances generally remember? This is a frequently used defense by subjects in criminal investigations. I'm amazed at how often criminal suspects can't remember committing a crime because they were too drunk. The next day they talk about the event with someone else or even try to avoid being caught by police and charged with a crime that they have told me they don't remember committing. If you are asking the person about a reasonably significant event in the recent past and you get one of the answers in the following list, you should be alert for other indicators that the person may be attempting to deceive you:

- "I can't remember."
- "I can't recall."
- "Not that I remember."
- "Not that I can remember."
- "I forgot all about it."
- "To the best of my memory."
- "To the best of my recollection."
- "Not that I can think of."

Denial Flag Expressions

These expressions are used when the subject is trying to convince you and himself of something. The key to these phrases is that they tend to help pinpoint the suspicious area. Just as when the utility company comes out to your house and sticks little flags in your yard to tell you not to dig here because of utility lines, these expressions highlight a sensitive area in a person's comments. The use of these phrases is saying in a subtle way, "You may not believe anything else I told you, but I need you to believe this." Don't forget that the use of one of these expressions does not alone imply deceit, but that we are looking for clusters of behaviors and behaviors that are a change from the person's constant.

This list definitely contains only a small sample of all the possible phrases a person could use, but will give you a good idea of how denial flag expressions sound:

- "Trust me."
- "Why would I lie?"
- "Believe me."
- "To tell you the truth."
- "Truthfully, or, truthfully speaking."
- "Honestly."
- "Really."
- "Frankly."
- "I couldn't lie."
- "To be 100 percent honest."
- "I'm telling you the truth."
- "I'm as serious as a heart attack."
- "I have no reason to lie."
- "I'm not lying."
- "To be absolutely truthful."
- "Let me be honest with you."
- "To be totally frank with you."

Modifiers

The best way to describe these words and phrases is that they are like escape clauses in a legal contract. When you first hear a statement you may not even recognize that they are there, but upon closer examination you'll realize why they are there. At first, the response you have gotten may sound pretty good, but you soon will learn that the person speaking has left himself a way to avoid being held to his response. Try these familiar examples: "At this time, I have no intentions of raising taxes on the hard working middle class of this country." Did you spot the phrase? Read it again and notice the, "At this time," at the beginning. What is tomorrow, next week, or next year but another time? See if you can spot the modifying words and phrases in the examples below.

- "I'm not trying to confuse you, but…"
- "I rarely make that mistake."
- "I hardly ever do it."
- "I was basically at home all night."
- "Essentially, that's all that happened."
- "He almost never does it."
- "Most of the time it works."
- "I don't think I could have possibly done that."
- "This sounds strange, however…"
- "It's usually on time."
- "He was sort of…"

Blocking Statements

The use of blocking statements by someone is a very strong form of denial. At just about the time you think you may have called someone's hand by pointing out some inappropriate behavior or deception, he will argue that your argument is in fact proof that he is being truthful or didn't act inappropriately. Here are a few examples. Notice they are not really denying what happened.

- "Why would I do something stupid like that?"
- "If I did, why didn't you say something before?"
- "If I were going to do it, it wouldn't be like that."
- "Now why would I do something that sick?"
- "Why would I lie about something like that?"
- "How could anybody get involved in something like this?"

Bridging Phrases

The name of this type of verbal behavior describes the purpose behind using the phrase. It is a bridge between two parts of a statement in order to keep them connected. This bridge spans the deep gorge in part of my story or statement that I would really like to avoid talking about. Have you ever had anything broken in your house only to discover that it was destroyed by one of your children? When you ask the culprit how the television remote control got damaged, you might hear something like, "I was holding it and just looking at it and all of sudden it stopped working." What you've not heard is that he and his brother were passing it around the room like a football when it bounced off the wall. The child has conveniently skipped over that part of the story.

Following are examples of bridging phrases:

- "Later on that day…"
- "The next thing I knew…"
- "All of a sudden…"
- "Out of the blue…"
- "Before too long…"
- "After a while…"
- "Lo and behold…"
- "Before I knew it…"

When you get an answer like one of these, go back and spend some time trying to find out what the person left out of the story. He has definitely denied you all the information you need to understand what really happened in the sequence of events.

Displacement

The use of displacement has been proven in research to be a frequent tactic of the person who is being deceptive. A general definition of displacement would be the inclusion of an increased number of references to others. If you have kids, you have probably had many of these used as an excuse for the child's actions. It's almost as if the person must create a crowd of like-thinkers or co-conspirators. Here are a few examples:

- "Everybody was doing the same thing."
- "All the other guys have done it."
- "Anyone else would have done the same thing."
- "They always do it that way."
- "Everyone has had the same thing happen."

You will want to be suspicious if you are asking someone about an incident and you hear this person talking about "they," or "them," or "everybody," or "all the others."

Stalling Mechanisms

Stalling mechanisms themselves may not be pure signs of deception, but they can alert the listener to the fact that a lie may be on the way. Stalling mechanisms give the person speaking the time first to decide, "Do I lie or do I tell the truth?" Second, "If I lie, how big a lie could I tell and get away with it?" If nothing else, stalling mechanisms are significant signs of forthcoming evasion and greatly signify the existence of mental stress. Stalling mechanisms usually occur at the start of a person's response to a simple question. Here are some examples of what a person using a stalling mechanism might do:

- Answer the question with a question.
- Repeat the question verbatim.
- Cough, clear throat, and take a big swallow or a deep inhalation before answering.
- Reword the original question by adding, deleting, or changing words.
- Pretend he didn't hear the question.
- Pretend not to understand the question.
- Ask you to repeat the question.
- Answer a different question from the one you asked.
- Insert a long pause before answering the question.

Surgical Denial

This is one of the biggest word games a person can play when he is trying to deceive someone with his answer. The deceiver deftly words an answer or response to an inquiry that relies heavily on the words chosen in their most specific definition or concept. After teaching this section in class one day, I had a student share a classic example of its use by her son. Mom had discovered that her son had been smoking and, concerned for his future health, she was trying to keep him from acquiring the habit. One day, the teenager came home from school and his mother said she could smell the smoke on his clothing. She confronted him with the fact that she could tell he had been smoking. The young man insisted numerous times that he had "not been smoking cigarettes." The tense exchange continued for several minutes with the young man continuing his denial in which he stated that he had "not been smoking cigarettes." It suddenly dawned on the mother what her son was saying, and she asked him, "Well, if you weren't smoking cigarettes then what were you smoking?" The lad responded that he and his friends had been smoking cigars, "But we weren't inhaling!"

Take a look at these sample questions and notice how the responses use surgical denial:

Question: "Didn't I tell you not to go to the dance?"
Response: "I didn't go to the dance with Bobby."

Question: "Were you there when Helen was talking about Leon?"
Response: "I wasn't in the break room when Helen was talking about Leon"

Question: "Were you alone with her in the office?"
Response: "What do you mean by alone?"

Question: "When was the last time you were at her house?"
Response: "I don't go in and I won't go in her house."

Question: "I thought I told you to come home right after school was out?"

Response: "I did. I got home before supper."

You have to listen very carefully to this person when he answers you because he is looking for that little gap or mistake in your question that he can exploit. One of the most prominent examples of this went something like:

Question: "Is there an inappropriate sexual relationship between you and her?"

Response: "It depends on what the meaning of 'is' is."

Remember to keep tying this new information into what was discussed earlier. You want to identify a person's constant or normal pattern of behavior when he is not under stress and look for changes from the constant of behavior that occur in a cluster of symptoms, because there is not any single behavior that proves a person is being truthful or deceptive. Remember, too, that verbal behaviors are only a portion of the total equation of communication. You should be paying attention to the person's body language at the same time you are listening to his speech symptoms. There may not be any verbal symptoms of deception but there may be visible body language clues. As with any other signs, make sure these cues are clustered. Body language symptoms are often the silent messengers that are telling you as the observer what kind of emotional stresses the person is experiencing internally and any disagreement or contradiction between verbal behaviors and body language indicate that the speaker doesn't fully believe what he is trying to communicate.

For example, suppose you have been working with a company for nine years and hear a rumor that there is going to be a supervisor's position in the finance department opening up soon. You'd really like to have the promotion; everyone else who has been there as long as you have has been promoted at least once, if not twice. You speak with your supervisor, and she assures you that you are being considered seriously for the position. Over the next several weeks you keep in contact with her, and she tells you that things look good for you. "Believe me, it's almost a done deal," she says. Your hopes are high as you share the news with your family. Then it is announced that a younger employee got the job. Even worse, you find out your supervisor, whom you have always trusted, had recommended the other candidate over you. "What happened to the done deal?" you ask. "Basically, it was out of my hands," she says. "You were qualified for the job, but office politics were against you. They wouldn't let me promote you because they wanted him instead." "They who?" you ask. "Upstairs" is the only answer you get. Who do you think really made the decision? When do you think the first instance of deception occurred? How soon do you notice denial being resorted to as a means to continue the charade?

In another example, a couple of city officials are accused of asking for and receiving bribes from contractors for road construction projects. A local news station has been able to break the story and even has managed to acquire some videotape of the meetings between the corrupt officials and the contractors to air. When shown the videotape, one official says that the contractors never handed him any money at any time. Later it's discovered that the money was always left under the front seat of his car in the parking garage. Well, he wasn't handed the money was he? When he is confronted with the public's knowledge of this information, he is asked if he thought it was wrong to take money from a contractor bidding on city road projects. He responds, "That depends on what you mean by 'wrong.'"

One thing to keep in mind when dealing with denial or any of the other response behaviors is that we cannot predict what the other person will do when he moves out of his current response behavior. For example, if you successfully disable another person's denial, he may resort to anger as his next response or just as easily divert his energies to bargaining. The ideal transition is for the other person to move into acceptance, but there are no guarantees for getting that reaction. However, you should be persistent in your efforts to uncover the truth. Often, this means you will have to adjust your own behavior numerous times to correlate with the other person's changing response behaviors. On a single topic, we may do this dance of reactions during one short encounter or conversation, or we may engage in it repeatedly over a longer period of time throughout our relationship as we deal with some difficult issue. For this reason, it is impossible to predict what the other person is going to do, and we cannot assign a specific sequence of reactions for response behaviors. Each person's response and response sequence to stress and confrontation is unique to the point that someone may not make the same response behavior transition he made in a similar situation in the past.

Each of the response states requires a specific reaction from you if it is to be dealt with effectively. With the bargaining response, we learned that in order to undo the deceptive nature of the response, it was best for us to temporarily agree with the disguise of reality. We should not allow ourselves to succumb to the hypnotic nature of the disguise as portrayed by the person who intends to deceive us. For the short-term, however, we do play along with the deceit. When the time is right, we call the other person's bluff by presenting the evidence from our observations. Hopefully, the other person moves into the acceptance response and brings openness and honesty to the communication and our relationship. On the other hand, the appropriate reaction to the denial response is to attack the deception with reality.

Remember that denial is the rejection of reality; therefore, you should attack it with the very element of evidence that the liar wishes to discredit or discount. For example, if the person denies being at a certain place, give the names of people who saw him there and remind him that he has gone to the place frequently in the past.

Perhaps there is some physical evidence, such as the stub of a movie ticket, you can use to confront him. Maybe he mentioned his plans before the fact or told someone else afterwards about the good time he had. Inform him that those comments to a third party have been shared with you. Alternatively, turn his explanation of the lie against him in such a way that he must either change his story or admit the truth. He says he stayed home all evening, but when you called, there was no answer. If he didn't go out, why didn't he answer the phone?

Nonverbal Signals of Denial

There is only one nonverbal signal tied to denial. One particular shoulder movement has been found to be a strong indicator that a person may be lying—the shoulder shrug. When you ask one of the employees you supervise if he is making progress on a special project and he responds with a smile, a "Yes," and at the same time a subtle shoulder shrug, that person may have well just been deceitful about his progress. A shrug of either one or both shoulders while responding to a direct inquiry suggests the person is in denial of the true facts. He doesn't believe or is not even really convinced of the accuracy of his own statements.[12] When you see this shoulder shrug, you'll want to respond by delving deeper and attack the denial, just as you would when confronted with a verbal sign of denial.

Anger

Anger would seem to emanate first from our emotional side. It is not an active form of deception, as bargaining may be, nor is it the heart of deception, which occurs in denial. However, we often attempt to support the emotional response of anger with cognitive reactions. This is the mechanism whereby I attempt to control or dominate a situation or another person. Oriented toward fight rather than toward compromise, anger is going to be about as far as possible from accepting reality. In fact, anger shows up when we are feeling over-whelmed by reality and responding with a strong survival mecha-nism. I'm also more likely to respond with anger when someone else has pointed out my failings and faults.

Anger creates a fortress mentality within a person. I am inside a fort and perceive that I am being attacked. If the enemy gets close enough and is able to test my defenses, he will learn that I am vul-nerable. To protect myself, I don't wait for the enemy to discover my weaknesses; I launch an attack that is designed to call attention away from my weakness and force the enemy to protect himself.

I may respond to a situation with anger for one of several rea-sons. I may be experiencing a great deal of fear. I may be in fear because of what I perceive as a physical threat to my safety and well-being. This is the instinctive part of my being human and I am merely trying to survive. This is the fight portion of the fight or flight mechanism I experience when I feel I am in danger. I also experience this form of anger when I am in fear of threats that I think are being made to my emotional stability. I don't want the delicate balance of my fragile feelings to be upset by facing an uncomfortable reality. It is not likely that the person who intends to deceive you is actually in danger of any physical threat from you. He is more likely responding to the threat to his emotional stability.

I may react with anger because I am acutely aware I have failed in some way or it appears I may be going to fail. None of us wants to fail, and the more we have at stake the greater our fear of failure. I may have failed to meet my own expectations, whether they are real-istic goals or not. Perhaps I have failed to live up to the expectations of someone else and that other person and his opinion may be very important to me. In any case, I will experience even greater frustra-tion and hostility if someone else is pointing out those failures or if I believe someone else is responsible for my lack of success. The fact that you are making me face the embarrassing reality of my failures will make you the target of my aggression.

My anger response may be triggered if I feel you represent a direct threat to my self-esteem. Your statements or actions appear to me to have the specific goal of making me look bad in front of other people who are important to me or to humiliate me so that I will be submissive to you. This usually occurs when there is some criticism of me directly or of my work. This type of anger may also be triggered if there has been a past history of bad feelings between us. These bad feelings may be the result of some previous incident or failure for which I consider you in some way to be at fault. Another contentious contact between us has opened old wounds as well as causing new ones. It takes a long time to heal these wounds and rebuild a relationship of trust, and sometimes it just never happens.

Note that a person who is responding with anger is not necessarily being deceptive. The issue itself is of great importance and concern to that person. He may decide later to use deception to protect himself from exposure, but anger alone is not a sign of deception. A truthful person also may become angry and frustrated upon not being believed. In such a situation, you may be contaminating the other person's reactions to your questions by expressing that you are challenging his

The anger response is not necessarily a sign of deception, but is definitely a sign of stress.

credibility. As we have noted above, if there has been a previous history of heated encounters between the two of you, the anger you are seeing from the other person may have nothing at all to do with deception, but may very well be a reaction to a poorly developed or dysfunctional relationship.

Remember that a person responds with anger when he is overwhelmed with frustration and unable to deal with the current situation. We discussed several key elements to anger that create major barriers to good communication. First, anger creates something of a fortress mentality. This person feels that he is surrounded by multiple problems that appear to have no solution. As far as he is concerned, he has no way out, and will be bound and determined to defend his position no matter how long the siege lasts. Second, people who are angry don't listen very well. This person is going to become so entrenched in his point of view that he will develop an attitude of anti-agreement, and will eventually begin to reject all other possible options for settlement regardless of how mutually beneficial those options may be for him and for everyone else involved. Finally, anger totally consumes mental, emotional, and physical strength.

There can be several keys to defusing the anger of another person during interpersonal communication. The theories and techniques that exist regarding the handling of anger and hostility are numerous and very productive. What you should have as your goal is to defuse the current moment of anger and aggression during your immediate conversation. The first step toward accomplishing that goal is to remember the many reasons why this person has felt the need to resort to anger.

At the heart of the motivators that have a person resort to anger is that he feels both overwhelmed by his circumstances, and he believes that the situation is out of his control. The first approach you should take as the listener is to look at what topics are on the table for discussion and realize that you are trying to deal with too many at one time. Break the overall points of the conversation down into smaller, more manageable issues. This will help the person recover some sense of control and he won't feel as overwhelmed. Second, start with those issues which present the least amount of threat to the other person's sense of emotional safety and well being. Finally, don't allow yourself to get pulled into anger because you are frustrated with the other person's hostile and negative responses. Just keep in mind that one of you needs to stay in control and in this case it needs to be you. If you allow yourself to become aggressive, then you are only going to fuel the other person's anger, which will rise to the next level of intensity. This will only be an even greater wedge driven between you and this person.

Verbal Signals of Anger

The anger response from a person does not mean that he is going to be deceitful, nor does its absence mean that the person is going to be truthful. A person certainly may use anger to avoid being caught in deceit, but a person who has been wrongly accused of anything significant also has every right to be angry.

As we described, anger results in poor listening behaviors on the part of the angry person. As someone who is interested in getting to the bottom of some issue or conflict between another and myself, I need to know when barriers exist between the two of us and resolution of our problem. I must be able to identify the speech content evidence that this person may be angry. Most of the time we think that the signs of anger include a loud voice, harsh facial expression, and aggressive nonverbal behaviors. Those are only the obvious symptoms, however. A person may respond to a situation with anger in a very cold, flat response.

The mental state of anger can be present when someone uses diffused or disguised remarks. For example, instead of addressing the specific issue you might have raised with him, he may complain about the fact that you have brought up the topic, or say that he doesn't want to discuss the issue right now. Of course, if you have brought up a sensitive or complex issue in front of other people or when one or both of you have time constraints, then it may be the wrong time to discuss the topic. But a person may be withholding critical details from you if he questions why you are making your inquiry as opposed to giving you an answer to your question.

As an investigative interviewer, I have always found it interesting when a person does not deny the fact that he has done something wrong, but instead attacks the facts contained in my case. These people don't deny they did the deed, it's just that, "You can't prove it." Think of how often you've heard someone say, "There's no real proof," "They have no real evidence," or, "You can't prove I did that." Perhaps there is a product on the market that a consumer protection group has identified as dangerous. You may hear the offending company defend their product by saying that the safety tests are not reliable, the results have not been reported accurately, the results have been misrepresented, or the testing agency was biased. Notice that they offer no alternate evidence and may even say, "Well, it always worked for us," or, "We've had no substantiated reports."

Other diversionary tactics that may be demonstrated by a person who is angry may be to argue about minor details or trivial points. I may insist the time or maybe even the date of a particular incident is wrong. Maybe the description of my behavior is not accurate. Maybe the number of times I did or did not do something is incorrect or perhaps the volume or amount of what I had in my hands, how much I spent, how much something cost, or its value becomes the point that I choose to argue about. I can find any number of unrelated issues to raise in order to avoid addressing the heart of the conflict between us. Remember that these forms of behavior by themselves are not a definitive indication of deception, but, if they are numerous and if they appear amid a cluster of other verbal and nonverbal signals, then they are a pretty good indication that evasion of the real issue is taking place.

Of course, an aggressive response by another person can be very personal. This response is obviously going to be very destructive of any effort to find common ground or compromise. If you ever read the newspapers or see news reports regarding people who have committed a crime, you have no doubt heard about the individual who blamed the victim for what happened. He should have not been there at that time of night. The person was of questionable character in the first place or lived a dangerous lifestyle. What about the two siblings who have been in a fight? Invariably the parent who separates the two children is going to hear, "He started it!"

In the most openly aggressive situations, one person may verbally attack another in an attempt to maintain control and dominance of a situation he could feel is quickly slipping away. I may engage in highly intimidating verbal dialogue such as threatening to ruin your career or tell your friends something embarrassing about you. Following are several examples of this kind of evasive verbal attack:

- "Just who are you to ask such a thing?"
- "Is it really any of your business?"
- "You have no idea what I'm going through."
- "Don't even talk to me until you have to face the same exact situation."

As an expression of anger, you may be accused of not being impartial or that you are biased in some form and therefore your judgment is flawed or your intentions less than genuine. Here are some more examples:

- "You are just saying that because I belong to the union."
- "The only reason you're doing this is because you never really liked me."
- "You've always been jealous of me."

An excellent way I can get the upper hand is to point out some past error or transgression that you have committed and be sure to remind you that you, too, are human and are not without flaws. In all these situations, the real issue at hand is not being addressed and the attention of both persons is being distracted to side or even unrelated issues.

Other examples of angry responses that may be used to distract you may be found in the form of accusations such as:

- "It doesn't matter what I say, you've already got your mind made up anyway."
- "You're doing all this just to prove to people how important you are."
- "It's obvious that he is out of control."

- "They have always had it in for me."
- "I'm just a thorn in their side so they will try to ruin me."

Once again, remember that a person using anger is trying to regain control of a situation which he feels has gotten out of hand. At the same time, he may still be avoiding the importance of the issue itself.

Nonverbal Signals of Anger

There are a couple of positions of the head that suggest that some degree of hostility may be building within the person's emotional response. If the conversation happens to involve a controversial issue, you may notice that it appears that the other person has his head tilted up slightly, and it appears that he is projecting or even pointing or thrusting out his chin. You are now observing a person who is demonstrating aggression or experiencing some feelings of hostility toward you or the topic in general. It is not uncommon to see extremes of this type of head and chin posture right before the start of a fistfight, or at least a full-blown argument. Watch two players from opposing teams in a highly charged football or hockey game as they "talk trash" to each other and you are bound to see this aggressive head posturing by one or both players. The next action you may see them take is to throw down the gloves, yank off their helmets, and start exchanging blows!

There is another behavior involving the head and jaw that suggests that the person is experiencing some feelings of anger or hostility. In this case however, the person is working quite hard to keep his aggression under control. To spot this response, watch the back portion of both sides of the person's jaw—the portion of the jaw that is almost directly under and slightly forward of the ears. As the aggression builds and the person tries to control his anger, you may spot the flexing of the jaw muscle. This occurs because the person is clenching his jaw or even grinding his teeth. This is a sure sign of suppressed hostility and the person is doing everything in his power to control himself.

If you notice that the eyelids appear to be partially closed almost as if the person is squinting and that the eyebrows appear to have something of a "V" shape to them you may be seeing the development of some anger or hostility. You will notice also that the muscles around the eyes, such as at the corner of the eyes and the upper cheeks, appear to be tight or maybe even flexed. Do you ever recall as a child sitting in church with your parents but you weren't using your best church behavior? As you continued to squirm, whisper, fidget, sigh loudly, or even poke your brother or sister in the ribs, did mom or dad ever give you the look? You know the one. That look that said you were going to be in serious trouble when your parents got you home. That's the same kind of expression to a lesser or even greater degree that you are watching for as an indicator of stress or possible deception. This expression by itself is not a sign of deception, but only a sign that aggression may be building or present in the person's emotional response. If you notice that the person is smiling at you but at the same time giving you the look, then the person is not being genuine about his true feelings.

Should you notice that a person has his arms crossed in a very high position over his chest you can interpret that this person is exhibiting some very strong rejection regarding the issue at hand and is probably in a hostile frame of mind. This position might remind you of the child or teenager who is demonstrating defiance while arguing with a parent. At this point you are also probably hearing a significant change in the voice quality toward a more aggressive sound and the content of speech will be deciphered as anger. Another body language cue that is consistent with the response of anger or hostility is if you see the person has one or both fists clenched under his arms. If you get the sense that the person is hugging himself, be sure that this behavior is not a sign that the person merely is cold.

Finally, there are some hand behaviors that are good indicators of building anger or that the person in some way needs to gain control of the situation. The easiest of these anger behaviors to watch for is some form of drumming or tapping behavior. For example, you may see the person drumming his fingers as he waits impatiently for the waiter to return to the table and take the dinner order. Your boss may ball up her fist and symbolically or even physically pound it on the table as a sign of aggression. A variation might be to pound the fist into the hand, or pounding on the arm of the chair. Instead of using a fist, the person might substitute a chopping motion with his hand or hands. Anger is used by a person not only because he is experiencing anger on an emotional level at the moment, but also it may be a sign that he feels the flow of events is not to his liking, or he may feel a little out of control in the midst of that flow.

Another behavior that can be indicative of anger is finger pointing. That doesn't mean that simply pointing to someone in a specific direction indicates anger. This pointing behavior will have a strong and abrasive thrusting action to it. Watching someone from a distance while engaging in this behavior will make you think of someone who is stabbing at someone else with a knife or sword. The thrusting behavior may either be outward toward something or someone else or it can be gesturing back toward himself. The more animated the thrusting behavior, the greater the intensity of the person's anger. If you notice that friend of yours using the aggressive pointing behavior and you notice that the pointing is down toward the ground you are going to discover that the level of anger he is experiencing is way over the top. In some cases, this behavior can be seen in the moments before a person becomes physically aggressive.

Depression

The depression response that I am going to discuss is a reaction behavior and not the clinical form of depression, which is an affective disorder. The affective disorder of clinical depression requires extensive treatment and possibly medication, and may have long-lasting effects on a person's family life, job, school, health, emotions, and much more. The form of depression I am going to describe is one that occurs as a result of some recent event. It generally has a short lifespan and does not disable the person experiencing this emotion. In this case, the depression response is a form of isolation from reality in which a person is trying to withdraw from the uncomfortable circumstances with which he has been confronted.

Like the anger response I discussed earlier, there is an element of aggression present in the depression response, except this time it is focused inward. In this emotional flight response, a person withdraws into himself and finds blame in his own actions. He is more or less beating himself up from the inside. Since we each know our own self the best, we also know our own vulnerabilities and we focus our attack by highlighting or calling attention to our weaknesses, failures, misgivings, and disasters. The end result is that we virtually burn ourselves up emotionally and cognitively from the inside out. When a person has finally finished his self-destruction, there is little or no real energy left to deal with the main issue that caused the emotional collapse, so the problem or issue is left unsolved or unresolved.

The depression response is a reaction to behavior, and not the clinical form of depression.

There are several communication barricades that are created with this form of response. First, attention is going to be totally focused inward. The person will tend to become mostly focused on his pain and failure, and hardly at all focused on any issue that someone else wants to address. The end result is that the person seems to be ignoring all other outside issues that need to be addressed. As a result of this response, listening skills, just as in the anger response, are very poor. What little he does hear is screened to find only those issues that confirm his negative image of himself. This self-confirming state does nothing but drive the person further and further into withdrawal. Interestingly, the same triggers that set off an anger response also can cause withdrawal into depression.

Little or no deception occurs in the depression response, because the person is so concerned about how bad he feels or how bad he thinks he is. In addition, not only are listening skills very poor, but he will do a poor job of editing his own open verbal remarks. Remember, he has focused his attention on what he thinks are all the bad aspects of his actions and himself. He will have little concern about others hearing about them because he thinks they already know. As a result, he will be doing little to hide his actions or intentions from others. Putting himself on such open display does little to help him create and maintain deception.

There is one caution about the depression response. There may be times that the deceptive person will use depression as a bargaining response. He does not truly feel depression, but he wants the observer to believe this is what is happening. The hope is that the observer will buy into the idea that the person is depressed, and will have compassion and ignore the real issue—the deceit.

If a person is really experiencing the response state of depression, you are going to be able to recognize the response on three levels. First, you are going to "feel" his depression yourself. On an instinctive level, you will be able to sympathize with the person. Second, you are going to hear the depression in the quality of the person's voice and in the content of his speech. Finally, you are going to see depression in the person's body language. All these factors will create a cluster by which you can determine that the person is truly in depression.

Depression has almost all the exact same triggers as anger. This time, however, instead of attacking the problem, a person is attacking and blaming himself and is trying to isolate himself from the reality of the situation. Once again, this is not an attempt to get you to psychoanalyze the other individual and diagnose this person as having depression. We are discussing the reactive form of depression that occurs when the person is responding to a current problem, not the form of clinical depression that runs much deeper.

A person who is experiencing the reactive form of depression that we are describing has become totally consumed with himself. Because he has his attention focused internally, he is not very open to much, if any, new external input, which of course means that he is not going to pay much attention to what you have to say. What this person has focused on internally is the pain he is experiencing, and it is going to take up all his thoughts and emotions. If you as the listener ignore the pain or even dismiss it out of hand, this person may well swing back into a very destructive form of anger that can best be described as rage.

The best way to respond to a person who is demonstrating depression in his verbal and nonverbal behavior is to become passive and absorb his output. As long as this person is experiencing this overflow of pain, he is not going to be open to two-way communication. Draw the pain out of the person. Encourage him to discuss each of the painful issues that he is dealing with and allow him to describe the hurt that he is experiencing. Permit him to go into as much detail as he feels is necessary. Once he has dumped all the pain, then you can alter the topics and your conversation agenda. The key is to be patient, focus your attention on the other person, and listen.

As with anger, a person who is experiencing this reactive form of depression is not necessarily going to be deceitful. He may certainly withhold information from you because of the pain he feels, but he is not, as a general rule, going to lie. What you will discover, however, is that a person who is in this response behavior generally does a poor job at editing his comments. By being patient and listening, you may find that he will unwittingly expose what is causing him so much emotional pain. It is in these moments of unguarded expression that you will find pieces of the truth with which you can assemble a more accurate picture of the reality of the problem that exists.

Verbal Signals of Depression

The first thing we need to say about depression is that it is not a mechanism that a person uses in a specific attempt to deceive another person. It will, however, complicate the process of getting to the truth due to the layers of emotional pain involved. Depression creates some of the same problems that anger creates because this person once again feels that things are out of his control. This time, however, the person is withdrawing from the realities of the problem and he is attacking himself. When in depression, the person will verbally articulate the fact that he is experiencing personal pain and disappointment. For example:

- "This thing has really got me down."
- "I just feel totally overwhelmed with this whole business."
- "I just don't think I can deal with that right now."
- "I can't believe I screwed up so badly again."
- "I don't know why I even keep trying because I always screw things up."

If you remember our previous discussion about depression, you'll often hear that someone who is feeling its effects is focused mentally on his pain. Some people will inform you of all the other problems they are experiencing because of their depression. For example:

- "I keep making big mistakes at work and the boss has even warned me about it."
- "I haven't been able to sleep since all this started."
- "My kids have really been hurt by all this because I have been so hard on them."
- "I totally forgot that I was supposed to have that report in last week because I was so worried about this thing."
- "I can't even keep any food down because I'm so upset about all this."

- "This has been nothing but a big headache for me now for six weeks and I can't stop thinking about it."

Once again, this behavior does not mean that I am going to lie to you. It is a barrier between us in getting down to real issues. The listener in this case must be sure to listen to what is being said because it can generate tell-tale signs of a serious emotional state. In this frame of mind, a person may also make statements that indicate he may have thought about harming himself physically. Never take these remarks lightly. If a person starts making comments about harming himself, take those comments seriously and discuss it openly with the person. This person needs help and counseling. Work to put him in touch with a counselor as soon as possible and don't leave him alone until you are sure he is getting care.

Nonverbal Signals of Depression

Of course, not all behaviors are exact in their meanings and all of them are not perfectly clear cut in the way they are defined. Some of these behaviors can have contrasting meanings when displayed with other body language signals. In addition, we usually don't display only one nonverbal behavior at a time. Occasionally, you may find that one behavior has multiple meanings depending on the rest of the body language and speech symptoms. An example of one such behavior is when you see the person's chin appear to drop into the top of the chest or sternum. This position of the head has two possible meanings—depression or acceptance. For the investigative interviewer, seeing the person's chin drop into the chest along with some key verbal signals tells the interviewer that the person may be ready to confess to the crime. The same head position with different verbal cues tells the observer that the person is most likely feeling very depressed about the issue.

I would assume that you are most likely not interrogating your friend, spouse, business associate, or teenager about some issue. But let's assume for a moment that you and another person each have a very strong point of view or commitment about a specific issue. Each of you is adamant about an opinion and is trying to convince the other to see things from that perspective. Should you observe the other person drop his head into his chest or sternum and possibly give out a long sigh, he is mentally and emotionally seriously considering that you may be correct or is beginning to agree with your point of view. The key for you at this point is not to keep driving home your point. Be more conciliatory at this point and direct your remarks to how the two of you are going to resolve the conflict between you. You will be surprised at how quickly the two of you will move toward settlement of the problem.

On the other hand, a person who is experiencing depression may also exhibit the dropping of the head into the chest. This time however, the verbal cues will be much different. You may hear the person mention how bad things have gotten or that he feels responsible for the bad turn of events. At times, the person will even express that he is depressed or is feeling blue. Now is the time to focus on your friend's reasons for feeling depressed. Be a good listener and nonjudgmental at this point. This person doesn't need someone else to beat up on him, because he will be doing a good job of that himself. Look back at our previous discussions about the stress response state of depression and the multiple verbal clues that go along with depression.

Remember, sometimes to get an accurate reading of the person's current emotional and cognitive or mental state, you have to pay attention to both the body language and the speech symptoms. If the person you are observing is experiencing the personal pain associated with depression, there are several nonverbal cues that often accompany the verbal symptoms. We've already discussed some of the verbal elements of depression that included symptoms revealed in the quality of the person's voice and his speech content. The nonverbal facial cues can obviously include such things as the eyes being cast down or gazing down to the floor, corners of the mouth turned down, or the head dropping into the chest. It should be obvious to you that a savvy person who wishes to mislead his deception target can fake some of these symptoms. There is one nonverbal cue, however, that is very difficult to fake and oddly it is an expression or movement of the eyebrows. A person genuinely experiencing depression frequently demonstrates a subtle movement of the eyebrows in which the eyebrows move or more accurately twitch in toward each other just over the bridge of the nose. In some people this movement is so pronounced that the inner portions of the eyebrows turn up over the bridge of the nose. It has been found that this expression is very hard for someone to perform on command without experiencing true depression.[13]

If you notice that a friend or family member appears to have a slumped or a rolled shoulders look during general conversation, he may be experiencing some depression. Now this is not to say that everyone who displays this posture is a depressed individual, and the depression we are referring to here is not clinical depression, which requires counseling or medication. The depression described here is a reactive behavior. In other words the person is responding to an incident, conversation, or setting with depression. You as a friend or family member should be patient and provide that person all the time necessary to express his feelings.

If the arms are crossed very low on the body over the stomach, the person is withdrawn and may even be feeling some depression. It's almost as if the person is collapsing in upon himself as he attempts to withdraw or isolate himself from the current situation or conversation. When you observe this body position, also pay attention to the alignment of the person's elbows. You will most likely notice that the elbows are pulled in very close to the sides of the body. Another variation of this same image can be seen if the person is sitting in a chair. Instead of the person having his arms crossed low in front of the body or in the person's lap, you may see him literally sitting on his hands with the elbows hugging the sides of his body. If the person is standing in front of you, you may notice the elbows held very close to the body and at the same time the person may be clenching his fists. This is a sure sign of anger or frustration. On the other hand the more relaxed the person becomes the more the elbows will relax and will be held comfortably away from the sides of the body.

Another behavior involving crossing the arms is what we are going to refer to as "cocooning." This is an arm-crossing behavior during which it almost appears as if the person is literally hugging himself. Not only will the arms be crossed but they will appear to be almost wrapping around the person. This person is apparently experiencing a great deal of internal or emotional pain or depression and the cocooning behavior occurs because the person is trying to comfort or console himself. This person is going to be very withdrawn from the current conversation. As an investigative interviewer I have observed this behavior many times during interviews of people who have been the victims of some form of personal crime. I've also seen it from subjects who are withdrawn and depressed over the nature of their actions during the commission of a crime. If you observe this behavior in a person, try slowing down the conversation, take a very soft and patient approach and provide the person ample opportunity to express his personal pain. He is deeply involved in the pain he is experiencing and will not respond well to other issues until his personal pain has been expressed or resolved.

USING
what you KNOW

More likely than not, you have seen and heard many of the behaviors explored in this book. It is possible that you had already noticed that some of the symptoms have been significant indicators of a person's honesty about an issue. In some cases, you may have been surprised to learn that some behaviors are not reliable for identifying deception, or you may not have realized that other behaviors were significant. Needless to say, you have a lot of new information to digest, some old habits to break, and new skills that need to be honed.

Anytime we learn a new skill, there is a four-step process to developing and raising our proficiency in using that skill. The first step in that learning process is to demonstrate and explain the concepts and theories to the new learner. That has been my job throughout this book. You'll remember that we discussed the fact that there are some very important basic rules to correctly identifying and diagnosing the general honesty of another person's remarks or true intentions. These analysis guidelines are critical to maintaining, assuring, and improving the accuracy of your analysis. Let's review them briefly:

No single behavior, verbal or nonverbal, is going to prove that a person is truthful or deceptive.

Remember that you are not going to be able to safely identify truthful or deceptive behavior on the basis of one symptom. There has been no behavior identified that can be used reliably to spot truth or deception in all people.

Look for consistent *reactions to specific topics from a person.*

Sometimes people generate random behaviors. If the topic area is truly a problem for the person, you are going to see most likely a pattern for how the person consistently reacts to that topic each time it is raised.

Establish the person's constant *or normal behavior first, then look for* changes *in that behavior.*

Behaviors that are going to be important to your analysis are those that are generated because the person has experienced an emotional and/or mental change. In order to be able to recognize when those changes occur, we need to have a good understanding of what the person's normal behavior happens to be.

Diagnose behaviors on the basis of the presence of clusters.

Since there is no single behavior that can be reliable for diagnosing deception, you are going to make your diagnosis by identifying clusters of symptoms generated by the person. The possibility that two or more deception clues will occur at the same time as a random event is highly unlikely. Reading a person's body language, verbal content, voice quality, and any micro-signals all at the same time is far more reliable than using just one category for your analysis.

Look for contradictions in a person's behaviors.

Remember that whenever any of the signals from the four communications channels appear to be in disagreement or exhibit conflicting meanings, there is a strong possibility that the person is being deceptive. He is either not really feeling the emotions he is trying to express or doesn't believe that the remarks he is making are really true. The presence of these types of signals suggests a strong possibility of deception.

Be careful not to contaminate another person's behaviors.

Don't forget that there are two or more people contributing to the mood and content of the conversation. How you respond to the person and how you communicate to him has a direct impact on how he is going to behave. Inappropriate, aggressive, or threatening behavior or an appearance of being unconcerned and uninterested will affect how that other person is going to communicate. Is he reacting to you or to the topics the two of you are discussing?

Don't allow preconceptions *to cloud your judgment.*

You are going to make decisions based on your assessment of another person's behaviors. Be careful to avoid any bias or preconceived notions that might lead you to draw the wrong conclusion.

Cross-check your analysis before making a decision.

Did you take the time necessary to establish a *constant* of the person's behavior? Can you name the timely, *consistent changes* in behaviors that occurred in *clusters*? Were there any *preconceptions* on your part that would cloud your decision?

During our discussion, we spent a great deal of time exploring the different ways that all people react to the stresses associated with creating, maintaining, and planning deception: *anger, depression, denial,* and *bargaining.* Those people who are being truthful with us respond with *acceptance.*

Anger: People use anger to maintain control of the situation by trying to dominate. It is a response to the person's feeling overwhelmed by the issue, and its hoped-for effect is to discourage any challenges or questions relating to the problem area. The job of the listener is to try to defuse the other person's anger. Break down the issues into smaller points that will be easier for him to handle and discuss without creating the feeling of being snowed under. Responding to anger with more anger can result in a total communication shutdown.

Depression: Depression also occurs when a person feels that he is at the mercy of things he can't control. Remember that the presence of depression is not an absolute sign of deception, but it can create a strong barrier to open communication. This person has withdrawn into himself and is experiencing the emotional pain of self-defeat and perceived failure. Allow this person to talk out the issue and use supportive listening. Once he has dissipated all the internal pain, you will find it easier to discuss how to resolve the problem and any deceit that has been involved.

Denial: Denial is at the heart of deception. It is in this frame of mind that the person creates, perpetuates, and fosters deception. Your job as the target of this deception is first to isolate the deception accurately. Once you have identified deception, the only way to overcome it is to focus on the reality of the situation. This person is trying to avoid, discredit, or dismiss the truth and is trying to get you to do the same. Don't be diverted from what you believe is the truth. You may have to reiterate the facts repeatedly. Hold your ground and keep your patience.

Bargaining: Bargaining is disguising the truth. It is not quite the straightforward deception you will experience when facing a person in denial, but rather, it is more of an attempt at evasive lying. To accomplish this evasion, the deceiver will try to change your perception of who he is as the main character in the play of deception. He may try also to change your perception of his behavior by making it sound less threatening or inappropriate. He attempts to evade the truth and any responsibility. In dealing with bargaining, you will want to ask pointed questions and dig for very specific answers. Watch the assumptions you are making, and ask the person outright if these assumptions are correct. Then, he will have either to give you more information or to lie outright.

Acceptance: The person who is in acceptance is acknowledging the truth. In this case, you can use this period of openness to strengthen your relationship and express your appreciation to the person for being truthful. By doing this, you can encourage more open and honest communication in the future. Once you get to the truth with a person, you don't want to use it as an opportunity for punishing him for past sins. Punishing someone for finally being truthful with you is not going to encourage him to be honest in the future. Be compassionate and sensitive, not hostile and vengeful.

The next step in the learning process is to study what you have learned. We all have developed some bad habits in our communications with others and in how we have tried to identify deception in the past. You may find that you have to change some of the beliefs you have held in the past about how, when, and why people lie. Keep this book handy. I encourage you to bookmark important pages, highlight specific text, and refer to it often. When you encounter new situations, refer back to the book as an impartial guide to help you make your diagnosis. If you are inclined to do further research, I encourage you to use a library and look for scientific articles and studies on human communication and deception. These will help you to develop an even deeper understanding about the topics.

The next step in the learning process is to practice. Try making notes about your observations, particularly when you were right on target and when you misdiagnosed someone's behaviors. You are going to make some mistakes along the way. Learn from those mistakes and try to identify why you made them. Be sure not to cause someone else to suffer for your mistakes. Keep your observations to yourself. Telling someone else the behaviors you have observed while trying to diagnose his deception is counterproductive, can contaminate the current communication, and could put a strain on future interaction with that person.

When you first start to apply the techniques you have learned in our study together, don't try to apply all the principles all at one time. All these techniques take a little time to absorb, and it also will take time for you to become proficient at using them. Try applying a little at a time. Focus on one area of your observation skills and work on it until you improve in that area. Before too long, you may find that you are spotting those symptoms almost subconsciously. Once you have gained confidence and proficiency in that area, start perfecting your skills at spotting and defining another set of symptoms.

Finally, use the skills you have learned and practiced. It would be a wonderful thing if no one ever lied, but that, alas, is not the world in which we live. While you cannot stop another person from choosing to lie, you now have the skills to strengthen and improve your intimate, personal, and social relationships. You are now able to identify when a person is experiencing stress and discomfort in a conversation, and you know what to do to explore those areas in a way that brings deception to light, puts the person at ease, and restores openness and honesty. You also have the tools to modify your decision processes so that if you suspect deception in someone with whom you are in a social relationship, you can proceed with caution. You have developed and fine-tuned your ability to identify and disable deception and reduce the chances of being the victim of another person's deceit.

(A word of caution—you won't be able to use what you've learned in this book to become a better liar yourself. You'll simply have that much more on your mind, making your own deception cues more obvious.)

Remember that the proper use of all deception detecting skills and techniques is to make for happier and healthier relationships, based on open, honest, and direct communication. Go forth with the tools you've learned from this book, and build yourself great relationships.

End NOTES

End Notes

Guidelines and Basic Principles

1. Dr. Paul Ekman, *Telling Lies: Clues to Deceit in the Marketplace, Politics, and Marriage* (W. W. Norton & Company, Inc., New York, 1992), p. 17.

2. Allan Pease, *Signals: How to Use Body Language for Power, Success and Love* (Bantam Books, Toronto, 1984), p. 6.

3. Ekman, p. 65.

Verbal Communication

4. M. Davis, S. B. Walters, N. Vorus, P. Meiland, and B. Connors, "Demeanor Cues to Deception in Criminal Investigations" (forthcoming).

Nonverbal Communication

5. Martha Davis, Ph.D., Principal Investigator; Brenda Connors, Director; and Stan B. Walters, Research Consultant, "Credibility Analysis Validity Study: Nonverbal Communication Project—Final Report," John Jay College of Criminal Justice, February, 1999.

6. Ibid.

7. Neuro-Linguistic Programming and NLP are trademarks of Dr. Richard Bandler, and Dr. John Grinder.

8. Personal correspondence with Dr. John LaValle, President of the Neuro-Linguistic Programming™ Society, March 1, 1998.

9. Aldert Vrij and Shara Lochun, "Neuro-Linguistic Programming and the Police: Worthwhile or Not?" Journal of Police and Criminal Psychology, Vol. 12, No. 1, 1997, pp. 25–31.

10. Ibid., p. 30.

Response Behavior

11. Elisabeth Kubler-Ross, *On Death and Dying* (Macmillan Publishing Co., Inc., New York, 1969).

12. Ekman, pp. 101, 102.

13. Ibid., p. 134.

BIBLIOGRAPHY

Bibliography

Argyle, M. and Dean, J. "Eye Contact." *Sociometry* 28 (1965), pp. 289–304.

Atkinson, Richard C., Atkinson, Rita L., and Hilgard, Ernest R. *Introduction to Psychology*. New York: Harcourt, Brace, Jovanovich, 1971.

Aubrey, Arthur S., Jr., and Randolph, R. *Criminal Interrogation*. Springfield, IL: Thomas Publishers, 1972.

Baldwin, Bruce. "Emotional Misuses of Anger." *Piedmont*, January 1987, pp. 13–17.

———. "The Stressed Mind: Pressure Can Produce Thought Disorders." *Piedmont,* November 1987, pp. 18–22.

———. "Keep Your Lid On" *USAir Magazine*, February 1993, pp. 16–19.

Baldwin, John. "Police Interview Techniques: Establishing Truth or Proof?" *The British Journal of Criminology* 33.3 (summer 1993), pp. 325–352.

Bandler, Richard and Grinder, John. *Frogs into Princes: Neuro-Linguistic Programming*. Moab, UT: Real People Press, 1979.

Beattie, Robert J. "The Semantics of Question Preparation." Academy Lectures in Lie Detection, 1957.

Benjamin, Ludy T., Jr., Hopkins, J. Roy, and Nation, Jack R. *Psychology.* New York: McMillan, 1987.

Bennet, P. J. "Interviewing Witnesses and Victim for the Purpose of Obtaining a Statement." *Journal of Forensic Identification* 46.3 (1996), pp. 349–366.

Bilodeau, Lorraine *The Anger Workbook*. Center City: MN: Hazelden Foundation, 1994.

Birdwhitsell, R. L. *Introduction to Kinesics: An Annotation System for Analysis of Body Motion and Gestures*. KY: University of Louisville Press, 1952.

———. *Kinesics and Context: Essays on Body Motion and Communication*. PA: University of Philadelphia Press, 1970.

Bower, Gordon H. "Mood and Memory." *American Psychologist* 36.2 (1991), pp. 129–148.

Brown, Roger and Kulik, James. "Flashbulb Memories." *Cognition 5* (1977), pp. 73–79.

Buckwalter, Art. *Interviews and Interrogations*. Boston, MA: Butterworth, 1983.

Buffington, Perry. *Your Behavior Is Showing*. Atlanta, GA: Peachtree Publishers, 1989.

Buller, David B., Strzyzewski, Krystyna D., and Comstock, Jamie. "Interpersonal Deception: Deceiver's Reactions to Receivers' Suspicions and Probing." *Communication Monographs* 58 (March 1991), pp. 1–24.

Callum, Myles. *Body Talk*. New York: Bantam Books, 1972.

Campbell, Joseph. *The Portable Jung*. New York: Viking Press, 1971.

Cleckly, Hervy. *The Mask of Sanity*, fifth edition. St. Louis, MO: C. V. Mosby Company, 1988.

Cohen, Herb. *You Can Negotiate Anything*. Secaucus, NJ: L. Stuart Press, 1980.

Darwin, Charles. *The Expression of the Emotions in Man and Animals*. New York: D. Appleton & Co., 1872.

Davidson, Gerald C. and Neale, John M. *Abnormal Psychology*. New York: John Wiley & Sons, 1982.

Davis, Flora. *Inside Intuition: What We Know about Nonverbal Communication*. New York: New American Library, 1987.

Davis, Martha and Hadiks, Dean. "Demeanor and Credibility." *Semiotica* 106.1–2 (1995), pp. 5–54.

Davis, Martha. "Credibility Analysis Nonverbal Microcoding Guide." Unpublished Guidebook, 1998.

Davis, Martha, Connors, Brenda, and Walters, Stan B. "Credibility Analysis Validity Study: Nonverbal Communication Project— Final Report." John Jay College of Criminal Justice, February 1999.

Davis, M., Walters, S. B., Vorus, N., Meiland, P., and Connors, B. "Demeanor Cues to Deception in Criminal Investigations." Forthcoming.

DeTurck, Mark A. and Miller, Gerald R. "Deception and Arousal: Isolating the Behavioral Correlates of Deception." *Human Communication Research* 12.2 (winter 1985), pp. 181–201.

Dillingham II, Christopher R. "Would Pinocchio's Eye Have Revealed His Lies? A Research Experiment Using Eye Movements to Detect Deception." Master Thesis, University of Central Florida, summer 1998.

Ekman, Paul. "Nonverbal Leakage and Clues to Deception." *Psychiatry* 32 (1969), pp. 88–105.

———. *Telling Lies: Clues to Deceit in the Marketplace, Politics and Marriage*. New York: Norton Publishers, 1992.

Ekman, Paul, and Friesen, W. V. *Unmasking the Face*. Lexington, MA: Lexington Books, 1975.

Ekman, Paul, Friesen, Wallace, and Scherer, K. R. "Body Movement and Voice Pitch in Deceptive Interaction." *Semiotica* 16 (1976), pp. 23–27.

Ekman, Paul, and O'Sullivan, Maureen. "Who Can Catch a Liar?" *American Psychologist* 46 (1991), pp. 913–920, 1991.

Exline, R. and Eldridge, C. "Effects of Two Patterns of a Speaker's Visual Behavior upon the Perception of the Authority of His Verbal Message." Paper presented to the Eastern Psychological Association, Boston, MA, 1967.

Exline, R. and Winters, L. "Affective Relations and Mutual Glances in Dyads." *Affect, Cognition and Personality*, 1965.

Fast, Julius. *Body Language*. New York: M. Evans & Co., Inc., 1970.

———. *The Body Language of Sex Power and Aggression*. New York: M. Evans & Co., Inc., 1977.

Fisher, Ronald P., Geilselman, R. Edward, and Raymond, David S. "Critical Analysis of Police Interview Techniques." *Journal for Police Science and Administration* 13.33 (1987), pp. 177–185.

Fisher, Ronald P. and Geilselman, R. Edward. *Memory-Enhancing Techniques for Investigative Interviewing: The Cognitive Interview*. Springfield, IL: Charles C. Thomas, 1992.

Foster, D. Glenn and Marshall, *Mary. How Can I Get Through to You*. New York: Hyperion Press, 1994.

———. "How to Tell If He Is Lying to You." *Good Housekeeping*, June 1994.

Frith, Uta. "Autism" *Scientific American: Mysteries of the Mind* 7.1 (1997), 92–98.

Gazzaniga, Michael S. "The Split Brain Revisited." *Scientific American*, July 1998, pp. 50–55.

Gerber, Samuel and Schroeder, Oliver, Jr., eds. *Criminal Investigation and Interrogation*. Cincinnati, OH: W. H. Anderson, Co., 1965.

Gorden, R. *Interviewing: Strategy, Techniques and Tactics*. Homewood, IL: Dorsey Press, 1975.

Gray, Jeffery. *The Psychology of Fear and Stress*. New York: McGraw-Hill, 1971.

Greenwood, Peter W. "The Rand Corporation Study: Its Findings and Impacts to Date." Santa Monica, CA: The Rand Corporation, July, 1979.

Gudjonsson, Gisli H. *The Psychology of Interrogations, Confessions and Testimony*. New York: John Wiley & Sons, 1992.

Gudjonsson, Gisli, & Lebeque, B. "Psychological and psychiatric aspects of a coerced-internalized false confession," *Journal of Forensic Science and Sociology*, 1989, vol. 29, pp. 261–269.

Hall, Edward T. *The Silent Language*, Double Day, Garden City, New York, 1973.

Hare, Robert D. *Without Conscience: The Disturbing World of the Psychopaths Among Us*, Pocket Books, New York, 1993.

Hess, E. H. "The Role of Pupil Size in Communication," *Scientific American*, 1975, vol. 223, pp. 110–112.

Hess, John "The Myths of Interviewing," *FBI Law Enforcement Bulletin*, July, 1989, pp. 14–16.

Hocking, John & Leathers, Dale "Nonverbal Indicators of Deception: A New Theoretical Perspective," *Communication Monograph*, 1980, Vol. 47, pp. 119–131.

Hocking, John E., Bauchner, Joyce, Kaminski, Edmund P., Miller, Gerald R., "Detecting Deceptive Communication From Verbal, Visual, and Paralinguistic Cues," *Human Communication Research*, Vol. 6, No.1, Fall 1979, pp. 33–46.

Horvath, Frank S. "Verbal and Non-verbal Clues in Truth and Deception," *Journal of Police Science and Administration*, 1973, vol. 1, no. 2.

Hurley, Kathleen & Dobson, Theodore *My Best Self: Using the Enneagram to Free the Soul*, Harper, New York, 1993.

Irving, B. "Police Interrogation, A Case Study Of Current Practice," Research Studies No. 2, HMSO, London, 1980.

Irving, B. L. and McKenzie, I. K. "Police Interrogation: The Effects of the Police and Criminal Evidence Act," The Police Foundation: London, 1989.

Kalin, Ned H. "The Neurobiology of Fear," *Scientific American: Mysteries of the Mind*, Volume 7, Number 1, 1997, pp. 76–83.

Keirsey, David & Bates, Marilyn *Please Understand Me: Character & Temperament Types*, Promethian Nemesis, Delmar, CA, 1984.

Knapp, Mark L. *Non-verbal Communication In Human Interaction*, Hold, Rinehart, Winston, New York, 1978.

Kroeger, Otto, & Thuesen, Janet M. *Type Talk*, Delacourte Press, New York, 1988.

Kubler-Ross, Elisabeth *On Death and Dying*, McMillan, New York, 1969.

LeDoux, Joseph E. "Emotion, Memory and the Brain," *Scientific American: Mysteries of the Mind*, Volume 7, Number 1, 1997, pp. 68–75.

Leo, Richard A. "Inside The Interrogation Room," *The Journal of Criminal Law and Criminology*, Volume 86, Number 2, February, 1996, pp. 266–303.

Leshner, Dr. Alan I. "Addiction Is A Brain Disease–and It Matters," *National Institute of Justice Journal*, October 1998, pp. 2–6.

Leutwyler, Kristin "Depression's Double Standard," *Scientific American: Mysteries of the Mind*, Volume 7, Number 1, 1997, pp. 53–54.

Link, Frederick C. "Behavior Analysis in Interrogation," *Military Police Law Enforcement Journal*, Winter, 1976.

Link, Frederick C. & Foster, D. Glenn *The Kinesic Interview Technique*, Atlanta, 1980.

Lykken, David Thoreson *A Tremor In The Blood*, McGraw Hill Publishing, New York, 1981.

Marshal, Keith "Unmasking the Truth," *Security Management,* 1985, vol. 29 (no. 1), 34–36.

Marston, William M. *Emotions Of Normal People*, Paul, Trench, Trubriar & Co., Ltd., New York. 1928.

McNeil, Elton B. *The Psychology of Being Human*, Harper Row Publishers, New York, 1974.

Mehrabian, Albert *Nonverbal Communication*, Aldine - Atherton, Chicago, 1972.

Miller, Gerald R., Stiff, James B., *Deception Communication*, Sage Publications, Newbury Park, 1993.

Mobbs, N. "Eye Contact In Relation To Social Introversion / Extroversion," *British Journal of Social and Clinical Psychology*, 1968, vol. 7, pp. 305–306.

Molloy, John T. *Dress For Success*, P. H. Wyden, New York, 1975.

———. *Live For Success*, P. H. Wyden, New York, 1981.

Moore, R.T. and Gilliland, A. R. "The Measurement of Aggressiveness" *Journal of Applied Psychology*, 1921, vol. 5, pp. 97–118.

Morris, Desmond *The Naked Ape: A Zoologist's Study of the Human Animal*, McGraw -Hill, New York, 1967.

———. *Manwatching: A Field Guide to Human Behavior*, Jonathan Cape, London, 1977.

Moston, S. "The ever so gentle art of police interrogation." Paper presented at the British Psychological Society Annual Conference, 1995.

Mullaney, Rossiter C. "Wanted! Performance Standards for Interrogation and Interview," *The Police Chief*, June 1977, pp. 77–80.

Myers, Isabel Briggs *Introduction to Type*, Consulting Psychologist Press, Inc., Palo Alto, CA, 1980.

Nierenberg, Gerald I. & Calero, Henry H. *How to Read A Person Like A Book*, Hawthorn Books, New York, 1971.

———. *Meta-Talk*, Cornerstone Library, New York, 1973.

Pease, Allan *Signals: How to Use Body Language For Power, Success and Love*, Bantam Books, Toronto, 1984.

Reid, John & Inbau, Fred E. *Truth and Deception: The Polygraph(Lie Detector) Technique*, Williams & Wilkins Co., Baltimore, 1966.

Reid, John E., Inbau, Fred E., & Buckley, Joseph B. *Criminal Interrogation and Confessions*, Williams & Wilkins Co., Baltimore,1986.

Royal, Robert F. & Schutt, Steven R. *The Gentle Art of Interviewing and Interrogation*, Prentice Hall, Englewood Cliffs, Ca., 1976.

Rubin, Brent D. *Communication and Human Behavior*, Collier, Macmillan, New York, 1984.

Rubin, P. N., & McCampbell, S. W. "The Americans With Disabilities Act and Criminal Justice: Mental Disabilities and Corrections," National Institute of Justice, Washington, DC, September 1995.

Samenow, Stanton E. *Inside The Criminal Mind*, Times Books, New York, 1984.

Skinner, B. F. *Verbal Behavior*, Copley Publishing Group, Acton, Massachusetts, 1952, 1992.

Stern, Dr. John A. "In the Blink of an Eye," Reader's Digest, April, 1989, pp. 99 - 101, condensed from *The Sciences*, November/December, 1988.

Strachey, James *Sigmund Freud: The Complete Psychological Works*, Hogarth Press, London, 1976.

Swidler, George J. *Psychology For Interrogation*, Beverly, MA, 1971.

Trankell, Arne *Reliability of Evidence*, Beckman (distrib.) Stockholm, 1972.

Trovillo, P. "A History of Lie Detection," *Journal of Criminal Law and Criminology*, 1939, Vol. 29, pp. 848–881.

Vrij, Aldert, Lochun, Shara, "Neuro-Linguistic Programming and the Police: Worthwhile or Not?," *Journal of Police and Criminal Psychology*, Vol. 12, No. 1, 1997, pp. 25–31.

Wade, Carole, & Travis, Carol. *Psychology*, Harper & Row, New York, 1987.

Walters, Stan B. *Principles of Kinesic Interview & Interrogation*, CRC Press, New York, 1996.

———. *Practical Kinesic Interview & Interrogation Pocket Guide*, Lexington, KY, 1996.

———. *Practical Kinesic Interview & Interrogation Overview*, Lexington, KY, 1994.

———. *Practical Kinesic Interview & Interrogation Student Workbook*, Lexington, KY, 1995, updated 1999.

———. *Principles and Techniques for Observing Verbal and Nonverbal Behavior to Determine Truth and Deception*, Laurel, MD, Johns Hopkins University Press, 1997.

———. Videotape interviews of inmates; Ashland Group Home, Kentucky Corrections Cabinet, Ashland, Ky., 1989, Bexar County Jail, San Antonio, Texas, 1995, Blackburn Correctional Complex, Kentucky Corrections Cabinet, Lexington, KY., 1989–1998, Fairfax County Jail, Fairfax, VA., Adult Detention Center, 1987–1999, Weld County Sheriff's Office, Weld County Jail, Greeley, CO., 1997, Eddyville State Penitentiary, Kentucky Corrections Cabinet, Eddyville, Ky., 1993, Lebanon Correctional Institution, Ohio Department of Corrections & Rehabilitation, Lebanon, Ohio, 1996, London Correctional Institution: - Department of Corrections & Rehabilitation, London, Ohio, 1988–1994, Lincoln Correctional Center, Nebraska Department of Corrections Lincoln, Nebraska, 1989–1997, North Dakota State Penitentiary, North Dakota Department of Corrections, Bismarck, N.D., 1995, St. Louis County Jail Annex, St. Louis Municipal Police Academy, 1991, Northpoint Training Center, Kentucky Corrections Cabinet, Burgin, Kentucky, 1987–1989, 1999, Ogdensburg Correctional Facility, New York State Department Of Corrections,

Ogdensburg, New York,1987, Rankin County Jail, Rankin County Mississippi, Sheriff's Office, Jackson, Mississippi, 1989.

Walters, S.B., Vorus, N., and Davis, M. Credibility Coding of Verbal Behaviors: Part I: Quality Coding from Tape and Part II: Content Coding from Transcript, unpublished Guidebook adapted from Walters (1996), 1998.

Weisinger, Hendrie *Anger At Work*, Quill, New York, 1995.

Yuille, John C., ed. *Credibility Assessment*, Kluner Academic Publishers, London, 1989.

Yuille, John C. and Cutshall, "A Case Study Of Eyewitness Memory of a Crime," *Journal of Applied Psychology*, vol. 71, No. 2. pp. 291–301.

Zimbardo, Philip G. "The Psychology of Police Confessions," *Psychology Today*, 1967, Vol. 1, 21–25.

Zuckerman, Miron, DePaulo, Bella M., Rosenthal, Robert, "Verbal and Nonverbal Communications of Deception," *Advances in Experimental Social Psychology*, Vol. 14, pp. 1–59.

INDEX

A

ability, 8

acceptance, 112–23, 169–70; nonverbal signs of, 120–23; verbal signs of, 118–20

Andy Griffith Show, The, 62

anger, 63, 112–13, 147–56, 168; nonverbal signs of, 154–56; reasons for, 148–50; verbal signs of, 151–54

arms, 94–102, 155, 163–64; hands, 98–102; shoulders, 95–98

B

Bandler, Richard, 87

bargaining, 112–13, 123–33, 169; nonverbal signs of, 131–33; verbal signs of, 126–31

behavior; change in, 37–42. *See also* change; clusters of, 42–46. *See also* clusters; normal, 34; response. *See* response behavior

Birdwhitsell, Ray L., 30

blinking, 93–94, 121

blocking statements, 140

body language, 4, 26–27, 30–31, 33, 76–79, 89, 109, 120, 144; arms, 94–102. *See also* arms; eyes, 87–94. *See also* eyes; head, 80–87. *See also* head; legs, 102–106. *See also* legs

bridging phrases, 140–41

C

change, 37–42

children, 15

choice, 7–8

clipping, 70

clusters, 42–48, 51, 55, 56, 72, 120, 167

communication, 44–45. *See also* nonverbal communication; verbal communication

communication disharmony, 31–33, 40

confrontation, 11–12

consistency, 46–48

constant, 34–37, 56, 67, 85, 92, 167; change in, 37–42. *See also* change

contamination, 10, 51–54, 57, 168

courtesy, excessive, 132–33

cross-checking, 54–58, 168

crying, 90–91

D

data, 54

debt-service statement, 119–20

deception, 2, 4, 6–12, 24, 94, 114–17; detecting. See detecting deception; direct, 14; indirect, 12, 14; misconceptions about, 25–27; motivation, 15–16; stress, 19–20

denial, 112–13, 133–47, 169; definition of, 135; nonverbal signs of,

147; overcoming, 135–37, 146–47; verbal signs of. See verbal signs of denial

denial flag expressions, 138–39

depression response, 63, 69, 112–13, 120, 156–64, 169; nonverbal signs of, 161–64; overcoming, 158–60; verbal signs of, 160–61; vs. clinical depression, 157

detecting deception, 33–34; guidelines to, 34–58, 166–71

dismissal gesture, 102

displacement, 141–42

duping delight, 33

dysfunctions, speech, 66–72; common sounds, 68; mumbling, 66–67; nervous laughter, 68–69; pausing, 67; sighing, 69; stammering, 66–67; stuttering, 66–67; unclear thinking, 69–72

E

editing, 60–61, 69–70, 77, 115

employees, 15

evasion, 12–16. See also bargaining

eye accessing cues, 88

eye contact, 26, 87, 93, 120; deliberate, 91–92

eyes, 87–94; appearance of, 89–90; blinking, 93–94; eye contact, 87, 91–92; Neuro-Linguistic Programming, 87–89; tears and crying, 90–91

F

facial expressions, 4, 82–84, 155

Fife, Barney, 62, 65

flight behavior, 107–8

friends, 15

G

gestures, 4

Graham, Billy, 128

Grinder, John, 87

H

hands, 38, 98–102, 156; adapters, 100–2; and head, 84; emblems, 99–109; illustrators, 99–109

Haskell, Eddie, 132

head, 80–87; and hands, 84–87; facial expressions, 82–84; position, 80–82, 154, 161–62

I

incomplete sentences, 71

intimate relationships, 21–22

K

Kubler-Ross, Elisabeth, 112–13

L

laughter, nervous, 68–69

law enforcement, 4

Leave It to Beaver, 132

legs, 102–6; crossing, 103, 105

lying. See deception

M

memory lapses, 137–38

micro expressions, 30–31, 33

modifiers, 139–40

morality, 129–31

mumbling, 66–67

N

National Organization of Victims
    Assistance, 113

negation behaviors, 84

Neuro–Linguistic Programming
    (NLP), 87–89

nonverbal communication, 76–110

nose, 86–87

O

omission of words, 69

opportunity, 8–9, 10

P

pausing, 67

perception, 33

performance cues, 92

personal relationships, 22–23, 116

pitch, 4

posture, 4, 106–8, 122

preconceptions, 48–51, 55, 168

prejudices. See preconceptions

public figures, 16

public relationships, 24–25

punishment, 32

punishment statement, 118–19

R

rate of speech, 4

reactions, 32, 83–84; cognitive, 32, 62,
    64, 78; consistency of, 46–48. See
    also consistency; emotional, 32,
    41, 42, 61–62, 65, 78

relationships, 21–25, 52.

religious statements, 128–29

repetition, 71

response. See reactions

response behavior, 112–64; accept-
    ance, 114–23; anger, 147–56; bar-
    gaining, 123–33; denial, 133–47;
    depression, 156–64

responsibility, 9–10

S

salespeople, 16

san paku, 90

shoulders, 95–98; body cascade, 97–98

sighing, 69

slurring, 70

social relationships, 23–24

soft words, 127, 131

sounds, common, 68

speech, 60; content of, 72–73; dysfunctions of. *See* dysfunctions, speech

speech content, 4, 30–31, 33

stalling mechanisms, 142

stammering, 66–67

stimulus, 39, 41, 51, 61

stress, 4, 17–20, 32, 47, 60–61, 67–69, 71–72, 76–78, 90–91, 103–6; emotional symptoms, 18; physical symptoms, 17–18

stuttering, 66–67

surgical denial, 143–145

sympathy, soliciting, 128, 131

T

tears, 90–91

teenagers, 16

thinking, unclear, 69–72

third-person statement, 119

U

University of Louisville, 30

V

verbal communication, 60–74

verbal signals of denial, 137–47; blocking statements, 140; bridging phrases, 140–41; denial flag expressions, 138–39; displacement, 141–42; memory lapses, 137–38; modifiers, 139–40; stalling mechanisms, 142; surgical denial, 143–45

vocal changes, 4

voice clarity, 65–72

voice quality, 30–31, 33–35, 61–65; pitch, 61–65; rate of speech, 61–65; volume, 61–65

volume, 4

vulnerability, 9

W

white lies, 2

about the AUTHOR

About the Author

Stan B. Walters is president of Stan B. Walters & Associates, Inc., which provides interview and interrogation services and training to business, industry, and law enforcement agencies throughout the United States. He also serves as a consultant to law enforcement agencies, prosecutors, and private corporations on interviews and interrogations involving active criminal investigations. He started his career as a civilian employee with the FBI and later worked for the security division of a Fortune 500 company and as director of security for a commercial bank. He is an accomplished lecturer, speaker, and instructor and is in heavy demand nationwide for his informative and dynamic training courses. He is also a frequent radio talk show guest throughout the United States.

Walters is the author of *Principles of Kinesic Interview and Interrogation*, which is now in its fourth printing. Part of the internationally known CRC Press series in Practical Aspects of Criminal and Forensic Investigations, this textbook is expanding in worldwide sales. Walters has also authored and co-authored numerous training materials, audiotapes, and pocket guides on practical kinesic interview and interrogation. He has served as subject matter expert on interview and interrogation to Johns Hopkins University in the development of a revolutionary interactive training CD for the U.S. Department of Justice and also has participated as one of two primary researchers in a credibility assessment validity study that was conducted at John Jay College of Criminal Justice, New York.

Walters is an adjunct instructor at Eastern Kentucky University College of Law Enforcement, an adjunct instructor for the Department of Defense Polygraph Institute, and a member of the American Polygraph Association. He has taught at state police, local, municipal, and law enforcement training academies in over forty-five states as well as at the U.S. Department of Defense, U.S. Immigration and Naturalization Service, Drug Enforcement Administration, the Texas Rangers, Bureau of Alcohol Tobacco and

Firearms, U.S. Probation, U.S. Attorney's Offices and the Federal Law Enforcement Training Centers in Georgia, Arizona, and New Mexico, and numerous other educational, professional, and criminal justice training organizations.

He received his B.S. from the University of Louisville and his M.S. degree in Criminal Justice Administration from Eastern Kentucky University. He is also a graduate of the National Crime Prevention Institute.

Walters continues actively to study and research interview and interrogation behaviors, strategies, and techniques and has conducted hundreds of prison interviews of subjects convicted of all types of crimes as well as conducting forensic interviews. His work has received critical acclaim throughout educational, criminal justice, corrections, and fire services communities.

Huntsman Photography